The   's of Tuscany

traditional recipes

EDITORIAL PROJECT AND LAYOUT:
Edimedia SAS, Via Orcagna 66, Florence

PHOTOGRAPHS: all of the photos are taken from the Giunti Archives/G. Valsecchi, Florence, except for those on pp. 23, 53, 61, 102, 109, 115, 121, 125 from Arc-En-Ciel/Giunti Archives.

The publisher is willing to settle any amounts due for texts and illustrations for which it has been impossible to determine the source.

We would like to thank the *Chef de cuisine* Carla Marchetti for preparing the recipes in this book.

Texts and recipes are taken partially from the book:
G. Pedrittoni, *Tuscan Cuisine*, Demetra, 1999

 Except in the case of sweets, the recipes are for four persons unless otherwise specified.

www.giunti.it

© 2007 Giunti Editore S.p.A.
Via Bolognese 165 - 50139 Florence - Italy
Via Dante 4 - 20121 Milan - Italy
First edition: March 2007

Reprint	Year
6 5 4 3 2 1 0	2011 2010 2009 2008 2007

Printed by Giunti Industrie Grafiche S.p.A. - Prato (Italy)

Contents

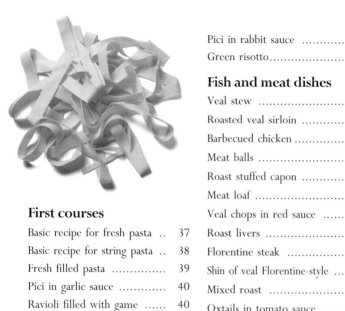

First courses

Fish and meat dishes

Eggs and side dishes

Sweet courses

STARTERS

Cecina
CHICK PEA PANCAKE

500 g of chick pea flour, 2 l of water,
1 glass of extravirgin olive oil, salt, black pepper.

Chick pea pancake is a typical, easy to prepare snack which lends itself as an unusual but tasty starter. Dilute the chick pea flour in the water. Leave it to settle, then stir with a wooden spoon. Add the oil and a pinch of salt.
Pour the mixture into a wide, low-sided baking tin. Bear in mind that the chick pea pancake must not be thicker than 1/2 cm, so if you haven't got a wide enough tin, it is better to cook two lots. Put the tin in a pre-heated oven and bake until a golden crust has formed. Serve generously sprinkled with freshly ground black pepper.

Striscioline
STRIPLETS

200 g of calf's head (or pig's), 2 medium-sized onions,
2 lettuce hearts, 1 green tomato, 1 medium-sized pepper,
40 g of stoned black olives, wine vinegar,
extra-virgin olive oil, salt, pepper.

This salad can be prepared using either a calf or a pig's head. Once the head has been boiled, cut it up into thin strips. Place these in a glass or earthenware dish. Sprinkle with vinegar and then leave in a cool place to rest for a while. Meanwhile, finely chop the onions. Wash, dry and prepare the tomato, pepper and the lettuce hearts, cutting everything into little strips. Discard the tomato seeds.

Add to the calf's head and season with salt, pepper, oil and a bit more vinegar. Mix everything together carefully. Lastly, add the black olives and serve.

Fettunta
TOAST WITH OIL AND GARLIC

4 slices of country-style bread, extra-virgin olive oil,
2 cloves of garlic, salt, black pepper.

Fettunta is wonderfully simple to prepare, its success depending largely on the quality of the oil. Ideally, it should come from cold-pressed olives. Toast the bread lightly over a barbecue (or under the oven grill).

As soon as the surface becomes crisp, rub the slices with garlic. Sprinkle with a pinch of salt and freshly ground black pepper. Then pour olive oil onto each slice and serve immediately while still very hot and before the oil soaks into the bread completely.

During winter, fettunta can be served topped with winter cabbage boiled in salted water.

Pane toscano (ricetta base)
BASIC RECIPE FOR TUSCAN BREAD

1.4 kg of bread flour, 60 g of baker's yeast, water

Tuscan bread, notoriously salt-free, is the perfect bread to be used for "crostoni" and "fettunta". Knead the flour with the yeast and enough water to obtain the right consistency. Knead the dough very well, then cover it with a dry cloth and leave it to rest for about 6 hours. Knead the dough again, divide it into 5 parts and shape them in the form of loaves. Lightly score the top of each loaf with a knife, bake in a moderate oven (220 °C) for about 40 minutes until the crust is golden and crunchy.

Totani in insalata
SQUID SALAD

500 g fresh squid, 1 bunch radishes, 2 carrots,
3 stalks white celery, 1 stalk green celery, 1/2 fennel,
1/2 onion, 1 leek, 1 bay leaf, extra-virgin olive oil,
salt, whole black pepper.

Wash the squid and boil in lightly salted water with the green celery, the onion and the bay leaf. When they are cooked, drain and cut into strips. Put these strips into a large terrine. Clean and wash the remaining vegetables. Slice the white celery, the fennel, the carrots and the white part of the leek but leave the radishes whole.

Stir the vegetables and the squid together gently. Season with salt and freshly ground pepper and plenty of extra-virgin olive oil.

Crostoni con funghi
MUSHROOM CROÛTONS

650 g cep mushrooms, 1 clove of garlic,
1 small onion, a handful of fresh parsley,
1 tablespoon of capers preserved in salt, 1 cup of stock, 1 tablespoon
of butter, 16 slices of country-style bread, 1 tablespoon extra-virgin
olive oil, salt, pepper.

Clean the mushrooms and rinse them quickly under running water. Dry them with a clean towel. Clean, wash and dry the parsley.

Then chop up the mushrooms with the garlic, the onion and some of the parsley. Heat the oil and butter in a pan. Add the chopped ingredients. Cook over a medium heat, adding a bit of stock if necessary.

Meanwhile, rinse the capers under running water and then chop them with the remaining parsley. Just before removing from the heat, taste for salt and pepper and add the chopped capers and parsley. Lastly, gently fry the slices of bread in a frying pan with a tablespoon of butter or simply toast them in the oven. Cover them with plenty of the mushroom spread. Arrange them on a serving dish and garnish with sprigs of parsley.

Crostini di fegatini
CHICKEN LIVER CROÛTONS

250 g chicken liver, 50 g bacon, 2 fresh spring onions, 1 carrot,
1 stalk of celery, 20 g of dried mushrooms, lemon juice,
1 cup of stock, parsley, 30 g butter,
1 baguette, salt, pepper.

Clean the spring onions, the celery and the carrot. Finely chop the vegetables and bacon, and sauté in butter in an earthenware pot. Meanwhile wash the mushrooms and leave to soak in warm water. Clean and wash the chicken livers. When the vegetables are soft, add the mushrooms, liver, salt and pepper. Leave to absorb the flavours for about 15 minutes and then add the hot stock. Simmer, stirring frequently with a wooden spoon for another 15 minutes. Slice the baguette into rounds. When the liver is done, remove it and the mushrooms from the stock and chop finely. Put them back in the pot with the parsley and a little lemon juice. Spread the mixture on the slices of bread, serve.

Crostoni bianconeri
BLACK-N-WHITE TOAST

50 g butter, 30 g parmesan, 1/2 tablespoon of chopped onion,
10 g meat extract, 20 g black truffle, 8 slices of country-style bread.

Melt half the butter in a terrine over gentle heat. Then add some of the grated parmesan and the finely chopped onion. In a small saucepan, blend the meat extract with the remaining soft butter until you obtain a light cream.

At this point lightly toast the slices of bread in the oven. Brush them with the melted butter and parmesan.

Leave to cool. Then spread them with the creamy mixture. Grate the cleaned truffle on top and then arrange the slices on a serving dish and garnish according to taste.

Crostoni di milza   ▶▶
SPLEEN ON TOAST

250 g of calf's spleen, 2 anchovies preserved in salt,
2 tablespoons of capers preserved in salt,
1 / 4 glass of dry white wine, 1 tablespoon of stock,
butter, extra-virgin olive oil, 8 slices of stale bread, salt, pepper.

Peel and slice the onion. Remove the skin from the spleen. Then clean, wash, dry and cut it into pieces. Next, sauté the spleen in oil and butter with the onion for about 5 minutes, preferably in an earthenware pot, stirring continuously with a wooden spoon. Remove from the heat and leave to cool a little. Remove the spleen and the onion from the pot and chop very finely with an ordinary knife or better still a mincing knife.

Put the chopped spleen and onion back in the pot and return to the heat. Add a little more butter and oil and stir with a wooden spoon until you obtain a smooth cream. Di-

lute with the white wine and then stir continuously until it evaporates. If necessary add a little stock. Cover the pot and simmer about 45 minutes. In the meantime wash the anchovies, removing salt and bones. Chop them together with the capers, which have been rinsed in cold water.

Stir carefully into the spleen mixture which has been removed from the heat. Toast the slices of bread. Sprinkle them with a little stock and spread with the mixture. Serve immediately.

Crostoni di caccia
HUNTER'S TOAST

70 g giblets from thrushes, blackbirds and snipe,
1 tablespoon of capers preserved in salt, 1/2 glass of red wine,
1 small onion, 1 tablespoon of butter, 1 teaspoon of meat extract,
1/2 glass of Vin Santo (scant), juice of half a lemon, nutmeg,
8 slices of country-style bread, salt, pepper.

Carefully clean and wash the giblets. Rinse them in red wine and dry with a clean cloth. Put them on a cutting board and dice together with the rinsed capers. Peel the onion. Chop and gently sauté it in a little butter. Add the meat extract and the chopped giblets and capers and gently fry. When they begin to brown, stir in the wine and season with salt, pepper, a pinch of nutmeg and cook until the wine has been absorbed. When it is done, add the lemon juice. Fry the slices of bread in a little butter. If you wish, you can sprinkle them with a little stock. Then spread with the mixture and serve.

Crostoni maremmani
MAREMMA CROÛTONS

*300 g chicken liver, 50 g minced pork, 1/2 glass of Vin Santo,
1 onion, 3 cloves of garlic, 1 stalk of celery, 3 sage leaves,
1 sprig of fresh rosemary, 1 carrot, extra-virgin olive oil,
1 baguette, salt, pepper.*

First peel the onion and garlic and clean the carrot and celery. Then chop the vegetables and sauté them in an earthenware pot with a bit of oil, the sage and rosemary. Wash and chop the chicken liver. Add to the vegetables together with the minced pork and stir them to absorb the flavours. Add the wine and cook with the lid on for 45 minutes. Cut the baguette into rounds. Roughly chop the cooked meat and then put it back on the heat. Spread onto the oven grilled bread.

Acciughini
ANCHOVIES

*Salted anchovies, large sage leaves, a little flour for dusting.
For the batter: flour, white wine, extra-virgin olive oil,
1 egg white.*

After washing the sage leaves, dust with flour. Wash, open and bone the anchovies, cut in half and place between two sage leaves pressing well so that they stick together. Prepare the batter with the ingredients indicated above, dip the sage leaves into the batter and fry in olive oil until crunchy and golden.

SOUPS

Pappa al pomodoro
BREAD AND TOMATO SOUP

700 g ripe tomatoes, 300 g stale country-style bread,
1 / 2 glass of extra-virgin olive oil (scant),
1 l of stock (light on salt),
3 cloves of garlic, 6 basil leaves,
salt, pepper.

This simple peasant recipe using leftover bread is undoubt-edly one of the most famous Tuscan recipes. Its success de-pends more on the freshness of the ingredients used than on the culinary skills of the cook. Highly nutritious, it is very suitable for children and is delicious heated up.

First, wash the tomatoes carefully. Then cut them in little pieces and cook in a saucepan over a gentle heat. When done, put them through a sieve.

Then slice the stale bread and toast it in the oven. In an-other pan heat up the stock, add the puréed tomatoes, the toasted bread, oil, finely chopped garlic, the whole basil leaves, salt and pepper and cook gently stirring frequently with a wooden spoon until the consistency is thick but creamy.

Remove the basil leaves, taste for salt and pepper. Serve into individual dishes adding a dribbling of fresh olive oil.

Panzanella
COLD BREAD SALAD

350 g stale country-style bread, 200 g fresh, not over-ripe tomatoes,
a bunch of basil, 2 medium sized fresh onions, 1 cucumber, red wine
vinegar, extra-virgin olive oil, salt, white pepper.

Panzanella is a traditional peasant dish which used to be eaten for breakfast or as a rustic snack. Cut the stale bread (preferably the grey, homemade variety common in the past) into thick slices. Place them in a terrine. Cover with water and leave to rest for about 20 minutes. Meanwhile, clean and wash the onions, basil, tomatoes and cucumber. Cut the vegetables into pieces and chop the basil. Place all this into a salad bowl. Drain the bread, squeeze it well, crumble it up and add it to the vegetables. Season with salt, white pepper, plenty of red wine vinegar and oil. Stir well and leave to rest about half an hour before serving.

Pasta e ceci
PASTA AND CHICK PEAS

200 g dried chick peas, 200 g ditalini (pasta dried in tubular form
about 1/2 cm in diameter and 1/2 cm long),
200 g puréed tomatoes, 2 cloves of garlic, 1 sprig of rosemary,
extra-virgin olive oil, salt, pepper.

Any kind of short pasta can be used for this typical Tuscan recipe or even long pasta broken up into pieces (linguine etc.)

Soak the chick peas in cold water for about 24 hours. Then rinse and boil in 2 litres of water.

Once they are done, remove some spoonfuls, and blend the rest with their cooking-water until smooth. At this point, season with salt and stir. While the chick peas are cooking, finely chop the garlic and rosemary. Sauté them in oil in a large pan. Add the puréed tomatoes.

Add the chick peas, both the blended and the whole ones, and stir well. Bring to boiling point and add the pasta. Serve as soon as the pasta is cooked.

Minestrone toscano
TUSCAN VEGETABLE SOUP 1

300 g short pasta or slices of toasted bread,
250 g fresh Tuscan beans, 150 g beet leaves,
1 slice smoked bacon, 1/2 savoy cabbage,
1/2 winter cabbage, 3 tomatoes,
2 leeks, 2 carrots, 1 onion,
1 stalk of celery, 1 clove of garlic, basil,
extra-virgin olive oil, salt, pepper.

Boil and drain the beans, retaining the cooking-water. Put half the beans through the sieve.

Finely chop the garlic, celery, onion, carrot, basil and place in a pan with the diced smoked bacon. Sauté in a few spoonfuls of olive oil stirring with a wooden spoon.

Clean and chop the other vegetables and add them together with the whole beans, the sieved beans and their liquid. Add more hot water. Season with salt and pepper. Bring to the boil and then reduce the heat and simmer for about half an hour. It is a good idea to protect the bottom of the pan by using a wire gauze heat spreader.

You can cook a small type of pasta in the soup or, if you prefer, you can serve it with slices of toasted bread.

Minestra di pane
BREAD SOUP

650 g fresh "borlotti" beans, 300 g peeled tomatoes,
70 g pork rind, 40 g bacon-fat, a piece of savoy cabbage,
2 leaves of winter cabbage, 2 stalks of celery,
a handful of parsley, a few basil leaves,
2 cloves of garlic, 1 medium sized onion,
slices of country-style bread, extra-virgin olive oil, salt, pepper.

Shell the beans and place them in a pot, preferably earthenware. Add abbundant water, cover and simmer over a low heat. When done, season with salt. In another pan, blanch the pork rind with the savoy and the winter cabbage for about 10 minutes.

Meanwhile, chop the onion, celery, 1 clove of garlic, the parsley, basil and bacon-fat and sauté in the oil over a gentle heat. When it starts to turn golden, add the chopped tomatoes and a pinch of pepper and cook for about 15 minutes.

When it is done, pour into the pot with the beans. Then add the pork rind and cabbage cut into strips. Stir and cook for an hour until the pork rind is tender. Taste for salt.

Now toast the slices of country-style bread and rub them with the remaining clove of garlic. Place a layer of toasted bread at the bottom of a terrine or a large serving bowl and cover with the soup.

Continue with further layers until the ingredients are finished. Leave this delicious dish to rest for a few moments before serving.

Acquacotta　🔜

VEGETABLE SOUP

*500 g cep (boletus) mushrooms, 250 g tomatoes, 1 l water,
1/4 cup extra-virgin olive oil, 1 clove garlic, 3 eggs,
50 g grated parmesan, 8 slices stale bread, salt, pepper.*

Clean the mushrooms very gently. With a small knife scrape the stalks.

Wash and dry and then cut them into thin strips. Heat the oil in a casserole and add the peeled garlic. When it starts to turn golden, add the mushrooms and season lightly with salt and pepper. Continue to cook over a gentle heat stirring occasionally with a wooden spoon.

Meanwhile, peel and chop the tomatoes. Then add them to the mushrooms. Add 1 litre of boiling salted water and continue cooking. Toast the bread. Then place it in individual soup bowls. Break the eggs into a soup tureen. Add some of the grated parmesan. Beat with a spoon. Then add the mushroom soup. Serve in bowls on top of the toasted bread. Sprinkle with grated parmesan.

Zuppa di fagioli
BEAN SOUP

250 g dried haricot beans (you can also use fresh "borlotti"),
350 g winter and savoy cabbage, 2 carrots, 1 stalk of celery,
1 medium sized onion, 1 ham rind,
1/2 glass of extra-virgin olive oil, 2 ripe tomatoes, some basil leaves,
8 slices of country-style bread, salt, pepper.

Soak the beans for 12 hours in abundant cold water. Discard the water. Put the beans in a pot and add sufficient water to cook them over a gentle heat with the ham rind. Meanwhile clean and wash the cabbage, carrot and celery, then slice them. Peel and chop the onion and sauté gently in a pan with 2-3 tablespoons of oil. Add the peeled and chopped tomatoes along with a few basil leaves.

After a few minutes, add the cabbage, carrot and celery and leave to stew gently.

When the vegetables are tender, add half the beans with a little of their cooking-water. Remove the ham rind and put the remaining beans in a vegetable mill. Add this bean purée to the soup and simmer for an hour over a gentle heat.

When it is done, taste for salt and pepper. Put a layer of bread slices in a large serving bowl. Cover with the boiling soup. Continue with more layers of bread and soup. Leave to rest for a few moments before serving.

Zuppa di cardi
CARDOON SOUP

500 g cardoons, 1 medium sized onion,
50 g bacon-fat, 2 tablespoons extra-virgin olive oil,
2 tablespoons butter, 1 l of stock,
1 cup of flour, slices of country-style bread,
salt, pepper.

Clean, rinse and dice the cardoons. Blanch them in lightly salted boiling water for a few minutes. Drain and leave to cool.

Meanwhile heat the oil and butter in a pan. Add the chopped bacon-fat and onion and sauté gently. Dry the cardoons and coat them in flour. Add them to the onion. Braise them for a few minutes. Then add a little stock. Simmer for a good 30 minutes.

At this point, put the soup through a sieve and then return to a gentle heat. Add another tablespoon of butter.

Taste for salt and pepper and leave to simmer for a few more minutes.

In the meantime, toast the slices of bread in a pan greased with butter. Then put them in a large serving bowl and pour the boiling soup on top.

Leave to rest for a few moments before serving to let the bread soften.

Ribollita

TUSCAN VEGETABLE SOUP 2

*150 g boiled white beans (or "cannellini"),
150 g boiled haricot beans, 250 g beet leaves,
250 g winter cabbage, 150 g spinach, 150 g carrots,
50 g celery, 1 small onion, 1.5 dl extra-virgin olive oil,
2 tablespoons of tomato purée, 2 cloves of garlic,
1 sprig of sage, 1 sprig of rosemary, 1 l of stock,
150 g stale country-style bread, salt, pepper.*

Peel and finely chop the onion.

Sauté in oil in a casserole, preferably earthenware. When it has turned golden, add the tomato purée and a ladleful of stock. Boil for a few minutes. In the meantime, clean, wash and chop the carrots and celery. Add them to the casserole and leave to stew over a gentle heat.

Clean and carefully wash the spinach, beet leaves and cabbage. Chop them up coarsely and stir in with the other ingredients adding a little stock.

Stew for 30 minutes over gentle heat. Then add the beans with their cooking-water and simmer for another 1/2 hour.

Lastly taste for salt and add some of the hot oil in which the chopped garlic, sage and rosemary have been sauted.

Then cut the stale bread into thin slices. Place it in layers in a large serving bowl and pour the soup over each layer.

Leave to rest for a few hours.

Before serving, heat the soup up again in a pan crumbling it lightly with a wooden spoon and season with a good pinch of pepper.

Zuppa di cavolo nero
WINTER CABBAGE SOUP

500 g winter cabbage, 50 g streaky bacon, 1 small onion,
1 clove of garlic, 4 large slices of country-style bread,
2-3 tablespoons of extra-virgin olive oil,
grated "pecorino" (according to taste),
salt, black pepper.

Clean and wash the cabbage detaching the leaves. Chop the onion, garlic and bacon and sauté in a pan with 2-3 table-spoons of oil. Add the cabbage leaves.

Cover and simmer for a few minutes over a gentle heat. Then add some lightly salted water and simmer for at least an hour.

Meanwhile toast the bread and place in a large serving bowl. Sprinkle with grated pecorino according to taste and a good pinch of black pepper. When the soup is ready, pour it gently into the large bowl. Leave to rest for a few moments before serving.

Zuppa di lenticchie
LENTIL SOUP

250 g dried lentils, 2 cloves of garlic, 1 stalk of celery,
1 sprig of sage, 4 salted anchovy fillets, 150 g fresh peeled tomatoes,
1 tablespoon of butter, 4 slices of country-style bread,
grated parmesan, extra-virgin olive oil,
salt, pepper.

Wash the lentils and soak them in cold water for at least 8 hours. Drain and put in a pot with fresh water. Bring to the boil, then simmer covered over gentle heat.

Meanwhile, chop the garlic and celery and sauté gently in a saucepan with a little oil. Wash the anchovies under running water to remove the salt, clean them, remove the scales and add to the well-browned vegetables, along with a few sage leaves.

Put the peeled tomatoes through a sieve and add to the casserole. Cook for about 10 minutes.

When the lentils are done, add a little salt. Pour the lentils and their liquid into the pan with the other ingredients and simmer for 30 minutes. Season with salt and pepper.

Fry the slices of bread in a pan with sizzling butter. Place them in individual soup bowls. Sprinkle with grated parmesan and ladle over them the lentil soup. Season it with a pinch of pepper and leave it to rest a few minutes before serving.

Infarinata
CABBAGE AND BEAN SOUP WITH CORNMEAL

450 g cornmeal, 400 g fresh red beans, 300 g winter cabbage, 2 pork rinds, 1 onion, 1 carrot, 2 cloves of garlic, 1 stalk of celery, rosemary, basil, wild fennel seeds, extra-virgin olive oil, salt.

Boil the beans in salted water together with the rinds. Meanwhile, clean and slice the onion, celery and carrot and sauté in a large pan with the crushed garlic and a little oil. When the onion starts to soften add the cleaned, washed and chopped winter cabbage. Stir and leave to soak up the flavours for a few minutes before adding the beans 3/4 cooked and their cooking-water. Taste for salt and cover. Simmer for about 1/2 an hour. At this point sprinkle the surface of the soup with the cornmeal.

Stir and cook for another 3/4 hour, stirring frequently so the flour does not form lumps. Serve the infarinata hot or cold.

Cacciucco alla livornese ➡➡
LIVORNO FISH SOUP

550 g cuttlefish, tattler, octopus, 350 g peeled tomatoes,
350 g soup fish (scorpion-fish, angler, swallow fish),
300 g mixed shellfish (clams, mussels),
200 g smooth hound, 200 g scampi and crayfish,
2 onions, 3 cloves of garlic, 1 stalk of celery, 1 carrot,
3 sage leaves, 1 bay leaf, 1 glass of dry white wine (scant),
hot red pepper, 4 slices of country-style bread,
2 dl extra-virgin olive oil, salt.

This is a typical recipe from Livorno which has undergone many changes over the centuries. Originally a dish for sailors out at sea, it has become the prey of land-bound cooks who have interpreted it in a variety of different ways. Cacciucco belongs to the large family of fish soups common to all sea towns. We need only think of the French and Corsican bouillabaisse and all the other recipes with their various names which are found along the Italian coast. One particular ingredient found in cacciucco is hot red pepper. First clean the

fish very carefully, removing the heads but retaining them. Remove the shells from the scampi and crayfish. Rid the shellfish of their impurities. Remove the eyes and beaks from the cuttlefish, tattler and octopus and cut them in big pieces. Put a little water in a casserole. Add the carrot, stalk of celery, sage leaf, bay leaf and a clove of garlic and cook the fish heads in it, strain; set aside. Chop up the onion with the rest of the herbs and sauté in a large pan. When the onion is tender, add the cuttlefish, tattler and octopus. When the juices have reduced, add the wine. Once the wine has evaporated, add the chopped tomatoes and leave to cook for about 20 minutes. Then start to add the soup fish and the smooth hound. Add the stock from the boiled fish heads, taste for salt and cook until the cuttlefish, tattler and octupus starts to get tender. At this point add the shellfish and the crustaceans. When the clams and mussels have opened their shells wide the cacciucco is ready. Arrange the toasted bread in individual bowls and cover with the soup.

Garmugia
RICH VEGETABLE SOUP

*6 artichokes, 1 bunch of asparagus, 150 g lean minced beef,
100 g fresh broad beans, 100 g fresh peas, 100 g beet leaves,
80 g bacon, 2 onions, 1 stalk of celery, 1 carrot, 1 lemon,
1 l of stock, extra-virgin olive oil, salt, pepper.
To serve: toasted rounds of bread.*

Clean and wash the vegetables. Cut the artichokes into quarters and soak for about 1/2 an hour in water and lemon juice.

Boil the asparagus in salted water. When it is half cooked, drain and put the tips aside. Boil the beet leaves. Then press the water out of them and chop. Gently sauté the finely chopped onion, celery and carrot in a little oil until tender. Then add the minced beef and the coarsely chopped bacon stirring it gently to let it absorb the flavours for at least 10 minutes. When the meat has browned a little, add all the vegetables. Season with salt and pepper and sprinkle with a ladleful of warm stock. After about 1/2 an hour add the rest of the stock and continue to cook for about 1 hour and a 1/2. Serve the soup with toasted rounds of bread.

Zuppa di funghi alla lucchese
MUSHROOM SOUP LUCCA-STYLE

300 g mushrooms (cep [boletus] if possible), 1/2 stalk of celery, 1/2 onion, 1 clove garlic, 2 tablespoons puréed tomatoes, 1 tablespoon freshly chopped parsley, 1 l of stock, grated parmesan, extra-virgin olive oil, salt, pepper.
To serve: 4 slices country-style bread.

Clean and gently sauté the finely chopped vegetables (not the parsley) in a little oil. Clean, wash, dry and dice the mushrooms. Cook for 10 minutes. Then add the puréed tomatoes and 2 full cups of hot stock. Add the chopped parsley and leave to simmer for about half an hour adding more stock if you think the soup is getting too thick. When it is done sprinkle generously with grated parmesan and serve in individual bowls over the lightly toasted slices of country-style bread.

Gran farro

▶▶

SPELT SOUP

200 g dried red beans, 100 g spelt,
100 g peeled tomatoes, 1 onion,
1 carrot, 1 stalk of celery,
1 clove of garlic, 4 basil leaves,
1 sage leaf, marjoram, nutmeg,
1 ladleful of broth, extra-virgin olive oil, salt, pepper.

Start the evening before by soaking the beans and removing the impurities of the spelt. Wash it in water so that the husks come to the surface. The next day, cook the beans in fresh water and then drain. Put the cooking-water aside and then blend the beans until you obtain a smooth cream.

Boil the spelt for about 3 hours. Clean and chop the onion, carrot, celery, garlic, sage and marjoram and then sauté them in a little oil in a large pan. When the vegetables start to turn golden, add the chopped tomatoes, spices, salt and pepper. Simmer for a few minutes before adding the beans and the spelt and their cooking-water. Cook for about 20 minutes stirring carefully. Add a little warm stock if the soup should get too thick. A few minutes before removing from the heat, add the chopped basil. Serve adding a drop of extra-virgin olive oil and a pinch of freshly ground black pepper.

See recipe p. 49

FIRST COURSES

Pasta fresca (ricetta base)
BASIC RECIPE FOR FRESH PASTA

400 g wheat flour (type 00), 4 eggs,
1 tablespoon extra-virgin olive oil, salt.

Pour the flour in a cone on the counter, leaving a slight depression in the middle, like a crater.

Break the eggs into the crater one by one and then begin to stir the flour in gradually until the eggs soak it up, taking care that the liquid part of the eggs does not leak out. Add the oil and salt and continue to mix, delicately at first with the tips of your fingers and then with a little more energy as the dough becomes thicker.

Only in cases of absolute necessity should you add a little warm water.

When the dough is of the right consistency for rolling out, put it on the pastry board kneading it more and more vigorously.

After some time the dough should become a smooth and even ball.

At this point, bring the dough to the "breaking point" by kneading it until, besides becoming smooth and uniform, it begins to stretch and swell here and there, forming air bubbles, as if it was alive. In this case it is better to divide it into at least two parts and roll out each part with a rolling-pin to form a sheet of pasta. Then knead it again and roll it out. Continue until you obtain a thickness of about 1-2 mm.

Then leave the pasta to rest for at least 1/2 an hour on a clean, floured cloth.

Then fold them and cut them into the desired pasta format. For fresh stuffed pasta, cut the pasta into the required shapes and place a heaped teaspoonful of the filling on one half of the pasta.

Fold the pasta over, seal it with your fingers round the filling and cook.

Pici (ricetta base)
BASIC RECIPE FOR STRING PASTA

400 g of flour (type 0 or 00),
1 tablespoon extra-virgin olive oil, salt, water.

Pour the flour onto a working surface.

Add the oil, a pinch of salt and enough water to incorporate the ingredients and form a smooth and very elastic dough. Kneed well.

Cover with a cloth and let rest for 20 minutes.

Then roll out the dough to form a sheet about 1.5 cm thick using a rolling-pin. Cut the sheets of pasta into ribbons about 3 mm thick.

Coat your hands with flour and roll the strips to round them into shape.

Pannicelli
Fresh filled pasta

For the pasta: 400 g wheat flour, 4 eggs, salt.
For the filling: 300 g fresh ricotta, 200 g boiled beet leaves,
100 g boiled spinach, 100 g bland, dry pecorino (grated),
nutmeg, salt, pepper.
To cook: 1.5 l of chicken stock.
To serve: fresh tomato sauce, grated pecorino, a little butter.

First put the flour on the pastry board. Add the eggs, a drop of water and a pinch of salt. Blend the ingredients well until you obtain a smooth, soft dough.

Roll it out thinly with a rolling pin. Cut it into rectangles of approx. 8cm x 15cm. Now prepare the filling. Chop the boiled beet leaves and the spinach and mix in the crumbled ricotta. Season with salt, pepper, nutmeg and grated pecorino. Mix carefully. Cook the pasta in the boiling chicken stock. Drain and arrange in layers in an ovenproof dish, alternating with the filling and grated cheese. Finish up with a layer of fresh tomato sauce, a sprinkling of grated pecorino and a few knobs of butter.

Place in the oven preheated to around 180 °C and gratinate for about 15 minutes until the top is crisp and bubbly. Remove from the oven and wait a few minutes before serving.

Pici all'aglione

PICI IN GARLIC SAUCE

400 g pici, 40 g fresh garlic, 700 g peeled tomatoes, 50 g grated pecorino, extra-virgin olive oil, salt, pepper.

First prepare the pici following the indications given in the basic recipe (see p. 38). Then peel the garlic. Chop it into slices and put it in an earthenware pot with plenty of oil. Sauté over a gentle heat. Wash, peel and sieve the tomatoes. Then add them to the garlic. Season with salt and pepper and cook for 30 minutes over gentle heat. Cook the pasta in a large pot of boiling salted water. Drain when still "al dente". Put it in a large bowl with the hot sauce and serve at once. Serve the grated pecorino cheese separately.

Ravioloni di selvaggina

RAVIOLI FILLED WITH GAME

For the pasta: 400 g wheat flour, 4 eggs,
1 tablespoon extra-virgin olive oil, salt.
For the filling: 2 partridges, 2 slices of smoked bacon, 50 g truffle,
200 g spinach, 100g parmesan (reggiano), 1 egg, extra-virgin olive oil,
1 glass of dry white wine, 1 sprig of fresh rosemary.
For the sauce: 40 g butter, 1 clove of garlic,
1 sprig of fresh rosemary, grated parmesan (reggiano).

Roll the pasta out thinly for the ravioloni following the in-dications given in the basic recipe for fresh stuffed pasta (see

recipe p. 37). Then prepare the filling. Clean the partridges and pluck the feathers. Singe the remaining down and hairs. Stuff with the bacon and rosemary and lightly brown in the oil, sprinkling with the white wine.

After cooking for about 1 hour, remove the partridges from the pan and bone them. Chop the meat. Carefully clean the spinach. Then blanch in boiling salted water. Press out excess moisture and chop. Blend the meat, chopped spinach, egg, a good handful of parmesan and the truffles cut into flakes. Season with salt and pepper. Place heaping table-spoons of the filling at regular distances on half the sheet of pasta.

Fold the other half over and press it down with the fingers around each heap of filling. Then, cut the pasta into 4cm squares. Melt the butter in a pan with a clove of garlic and the rosemary and sauté gently till golden.

Cook the ravioloni in a large pan of salted water, placing them in the water just as it is coming to the boil. When they are done, drain well, transfer to a serving bowl and add the melted butter after having removed the garlic and rosemary. Sprinkle with grated parmesan before serving.

Tortelli al cavolfiore
PASTA FILLED WITH CAULIFLOWER

For the pasta: 300 g flour, 3 eggs, salt.
For the filling: 250 g minced lean pork, 250 g sausage,
1/2 cauliflower, 2 cloves of garlic, 2 eggs, 1 sprig of rosemary, butter,
grated parmesan, salt, pepper.

Gently sauté the garlic and rosemary in a little oil. Then add the meat and sausage broken into pieces. Season with salt and pepper. Clean and wash the cauliflower. Parboil for 10 minutes in salted water. Then chop it into pieces and add it to the meat. When the cauliflower is well done, remove from the heat and add the egg yolks, beating vigorously in order to incorporate them in the mixture, which must be soft but firm. To prepare the pasta for the tortelli put the flour in a cone on the pastry board. Add a little salt and the eggs. Knead patiently until little air bubbles form on the surface of the pasta. Now roll the pasta into a ball, cover with a cloth and leave to rest for half an hour before rolling it out with a rolling-pin. Cut the pasta into squares and place a tablespoon of the barely warm filling at the centre of each. Fold the squares over diagonally to form triangles. Boil in a large panful of salted water. Serve with the melted butter and grated parmesan.

Pappardelle al cinghiale
PAPPARDELLE WITH WILD BOAR SAUCE

400 g fresh pappardelle, 200 g puréed tomatoes,
100 g minced wild boar, 4 cloves of garlic, 1 stalk of celery,
2 cloves, 2 bay leaves, 1 sprig of rosemary,
1/2 glass of red wine, 1 cup of stock, grated parmesan,
extra-virgin olive oil, red hot pepper, salt.

First prepare the dough for the pappardelle
following the indications given in the ba-

43

sic recipe (see p. 37). After rolling out the pasta on the working surface, cut it into ribbons about 1.5 cm wide.

Finely chop all the herbs and sauté gently in the oil with the whole cloves of garlic. When the garlic starts to turn golden, add the meat stirring it to absorb the flavours.

Season with salt and after a few minutes add the red wine. Lastly, when the wine has evaporated, add the puréed tomatoes and cook over low heat for about two hours adding a little stock from time to time to keep the sauce from drying.

Boil the pappardelle in a large pot of salted water, drain and season with the sauce and a good sprinkling of grated parmesan.

Pici al pomodoro, basilico e ricotta salata
PICI IN TOMATO, RICOTTA AND BASIL SAUCE

400 g pici, 4 ripe tomatoes, 1 leek, 1 bunch of fresh basil, aged salted ricotta, extra-virgin olive oil, salt, pepper.

Prepare the pici following the indications given in the basic recipe (see p. 38). Peel the tomatoes and cut them into strips. Clean the leek carefully and slice it thinly.

Then sauté the leek in oil until it turns golden. Add the strips of tomato and a pinch of salt and cook until it reduces slightly. Cook the pasta in a large pot of boiling salted water. Drain when still "al dente" and add to the sauce. Cook for 1 minute stirring all the time. Sprinkle with a generous helping of grated salted ricotta. Add a pinch of pepper and chopped basil and serve.

Rigatoni di San Miniato
RIGATONI OF SAN MINIATO

400 g rigatoni, 200 g puréed tomatoes, 150 g minced beef,
50 g bacon, 4 chicken livers, 1 / 2 glass of dry white wine,
1 onion, 1 carrot, 1 clove of garlic, 2 fresh sage leaves,
2 fresh basil leaves, 2 tablespoons of chopped parsley,
1 sprig of rosemary, 1 cup of stock,
extra-virgin olive oil, salt, pepper.
To serve: grated parmesan.

Finely chop all the herbs, using just a few rosemary needles and sauté them in an earthenware pot in a little oil. Wash the chicken livers and chop them up with the bacon. Add to the herbs together with the minced beef and stir very well.

Cook for a few minutes to soak up the flavours and then add the white wine and cook until it evaporates. Season with salt and a good sprinkling of freshly ground pepper. Add the puréed tomatoes. Mix well, cover and cook over gentle heat for at least two hours. If the sauce tends to dry up, add a little hot stock.

Boil the pasta in abundant salted water. Drain when "al dente" and pour into the pan with the sauce. Stir for a few minutes. Serve with grated parmesan.

Pappardelle alla lepre
PAPPARDELLE IN HARE SAUCE

400 g fresh pappardelle, 1 / 3 of a hare (including the liver and heart), 1 / 2 litre of red wine, 1 cup of stock, 1 onion, 1 leek, 1 carrot, 1 stalk of celery, 10 juniper berries, 2 sprigs of rosemary, a bunch of fresh parsley, 2 cloves of garlic, 5 grains of whole pepper, butter, extra-virgin olive oil, parmesan (reggiano), salt.

Clean the hare. Cut it into pieces and leave it to marinate in the wine for 24 hours with the onion, juniper berries, a sprig of rosemary, the grains of whole pepper and a clove of garlic. The following day, prepare the dough for the pappardelle following the indications given in the basic recipe (see p. 37). After rolling out the dough on a pastry board cut it into ribbons about 1.5 cm wide. Then remove the meat from the marinade and drain. In the meantime, chop the leek, carrot, celery, parsley and the remaining rosemary and garlic and sauté gently until golden. Then add the pieces of hare. Sauté them over a fairly fast flame for a few minutes, stirring with a wooden spoon and sprinkling with some of the marinade. Season with salt and pepper. Lower the heat, cover and cook for at least an hour, occasionally adding hot stock. Remove the bones from the hare and dice the meat. Then put the liver and heart through a sieve. Add all this to the sauce and return to the heat. Cook the pappardelle in a large pot of salted water. Drain when still "al dente" and add to the sauce. Stir them in for a couple of minutes adding a little butter. When the sauce is fully amalgamated, serve with a generous helping of grated parmesan.

Risotto alla toscana
RISOTTO TUSCAN-STYLE

400 g rice, 50 g minced beef, 50 g chicken liver and gizzard,
1 onion, 1 carrot, 1 stalk of celery, 1 cup of tomato purée, 1 l of stock,
1/2 glass of Chianti, grated parmesan,
extra-virgin olive oil, salt, pepper.

Chop half an onion, the carrot and celery and fry in a few tablespoons of oil. Add the minced beef, the chopped chicken gizzard and after a couple of minutes the chopped liver. Add the wine and cook until it's nearly all evaporated. Then add a little tomato purée diluted in the warm stock. Season with salt and pepper and cook for a few minutes before removing from the heat.

In another pan, fry the other chopped 1/2 onion in a little oil. Add the rice and stir with a wooden spoon until it has absorbed the oil.

Season with salt and continue cooking, gradually adding the boiling stock and stirring all the time.

When it is ready, add the meat and liver sauce to the rice and mix well. Remove from the heat and leave to rest with the lid on. Serve the grated parmesan separately.

Gnocchetti alla fiorentina
SPINACH AND POTATO DUMPLINGS

1 kg potatoes, 300 g spinach, 200 g wheat flour, 1 egg, salt.
For the sauce: sage, butter, grated parmesan.

Peel the potatoes and boil in salted water. Meanwhile, clean the spinach thoroughly and boil in salted water.

When done, press out the excess moisture and put through a sieve. When the potatoes are cooked, drain and mash. Blend the spinach and potatoes together, incorporating an egg. Add the flour and continue to mix.

If the dough is too soft, add some more flour to obtain the right consistency. Form the dough into long tubes and then cut it into 2cm pieces, place them on a floured cloth. Then plunge them into boiling salted water. As soon as they come to the surface, remove them with a perforated spoon, draining well. Serve them with butter melted with sage leaves and a generous helping of grated parmesan.

Pappardelle al fagiano
PAPPARDELLE WITH PHEASANT SAUCE

400 g fresh pappardelle, 1/2 pheasant,
1 small glass of cognac, 1 glass of dry white wine,
1 cup of vegetable stock, a bunch of fresh sage and a
sprig of rosemary, 60 g butter, 1 tablespoon of cream,
grated parmesan (reggiano), salt.

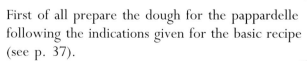

First of all prepare the dough for the pappardelle following the indications given for the basic recipe (see p. 37).
After rolling out the dough on the pastry board cut it into ribbons about 1.5 cm wide.
Clean the pheasant and remove the bones.

Cut into strips and sauté until golden with a few sage leaves in 30g of butter. Sprinkle with the cognac, then the white wine and cook until they evaporate. Reduce the heat, cover and cook for about 1/2 an hour, occasionally adding some hot vegetable stock.

Remove the strips of pheasant and strain the juices. In a separate pan melt the remaining butter and flavour it with a little rosemary.

Put the meat and the strained juices back in the pan, adding the butter flavoured with rosemary.

Cook the pasta in a large pot of boiling salted water. Drain when still "al dente" and add to the pheasant sauce.

Add the cream and mix well. Serve the pappardelle with a generous sprinkling of grated parmesan (reggiano).

Pici con rigaglie
PICI IN GIBLET SAUCE

*400 g pici, 150 g chicken giblets, 100 g mushrooms
(Cantarellus cibarius), 1 thick slice of bacon,
2 tablespoons of tomato purée, 1 glass of dry white wine,
a bunch of fresh parsley, 1 leek, 1 sprig of fresh rosemary, extra-
virgin olive oil, grated parmesan (reggiano), salt, pepper.*

First prepare the pici following the indications given in the basic recipe (see p. 38).

Clean and wash the chicken giblets. Dry them and chop into pieces. Finely chop the parsley, bacon, leek and rosemary needles and sauté them in oil till golden. Add the giblets.

Sprinkle with the white wine and cook till it evaporates. Clean, wash, dry and slice the mushrooms. Add them to the giblets together with the tomato purée.
Cook over a medium heat stirring frequently with a wooden spoon.
Cook the pasta in a large pot of boiling salted water.
Drain and add to the sauce stirring all the time. Sprinkle with grated parmesan (reggiano) and pepper.

Risotto con ragù di piccione
RISOTTO IN PIGEON RAGOUT

350 g rice, 1 pigeon (600 g), 1 salted anchovy fillet,
1 small black truffle, 1 small onion, 1 bay leaf, 1 sprig of rosemary,
1 piece of lemon rind, 1 small glass of marsala, 1 litre of stock,
grated parmesan, butter, extra-virgin olive oil, salt, pepper.

Clean and singe the pigeon. Then chop the anchovy (rinsed and scaled), lemon rind (only the yellow part), and the rosemary needles. Add the bay leaf and use to stuff the pigeon.
Season it with oil, salt and pepper, place it in an ovenproof dish and cook it in a hot oven (200 °C) for 20 minutes.
When it is cool, bone and chop the meat into strips. Put the bones and the giblets back into the roasting tin with the cooking juices.
Add a couple of ladlefuls of stock and a drop of marsala. Put back in the hot oven for about 10 minutes. Then remove the

pigeon from the oven, keeping it warm, strain the sauce, keeping it warm too. Clean and chop the onion and sauté in a little oil in a casserole. Add the rice and, stirring constantly with a wooden spoon, cook until it has absorbed all the oil. At this point, add the remaining marsala and cook until it evaporates. Finish cooking the rice adding a little stock at a time; 5 minutes before it is ready, add the pigeon meat and its sauce.

Remove from the heat. Add grated parmesan and a tablespoon of butter and leave to rest for a few minutes with the lid on. Just before serving, stir and add the flaked truffle.

Cappelletti saporiti   ▶▶
TASTY FRESH PASTA

For the pasta: 400 g wheat flour, 4 eggs,
1 tablespoon extra-virgin olive oil, salt.
For the filling: 250 g chard, 250 g parmesan (reggiano), 2 eggs,
nutmeg, salt, pepper.
For the sauce: 200 g chicken liver, 1 spring onion,
2 tablespoons of tomato sauce, 1 sprig of fresh rosemary, 2 bay leaves,
1 glass of white wine, extra-virgin olive oil, parmesan (reggiano),
salt, pepper.

To prepare the pasta, follow the indications given in the basic recipe for fresh stuffed pasta (see p. 37).
Clean the chard and blanch in boiling salted water. Drain and press out the excess moisture, then blend. Now put the chard in a bowl and add the grated parmesan, the eggs, a

pinch of salt, pepper and nutmeg, mixing well. Using a pastry wheel, cut the pasta into 3cm squares. Put a little filling on each. Then fold them diagonally into triangles. Seal the edges with your fingers.

At this point, join the two opposite corners of the triangle and press them between your thumb and forefinger. Leave to rest for a few hours. In the meantime prepare the sauce. Wash the chicken livers and chop them coarsely. Gently sauté the onion and rosemary until golden. Add the liver and bay leaf and sauté, sprinkling with the white wine. Season with salt and pepper. When the wine has evaporated, add the tomato sauce and finish cooking over moderate heat.

Cook the cappelletti in salted water, putting them in the water just as it is coming to the boil. When they are done, drain and pour into a bowl. Add the sauce, sprinkle with grated parmesan and serve very hot.

Pappardelle col cervo e funghi porcini

PAPPARDELLE IN VENISON AND MUSHROOM SAUCE

400 g fresh pappardelle, 350 g lean venison,
150 g cep (boletus) mushrooms,
1 / 2 l of red wine, 1 spring onion,
1 small carrot, 2 bay leaves,
1 sprig of rosemary,
40 g of butter, grated parmesan
(reggiano), salt, pepper.

First of all prepare the dough for the pappardelle following the indications given for the basic recipe (see p. 37).

After rolling out the dough on the pastry board cut it into ribbons about 1,5 cm wide. Dice the venison and marinate it in the red wine with the whole herbs and the vegetables for about 12 hours. Remove and drain the meat. Then drain the vegetables and herbs. Chop them and sauté them in sizzling butter in a large saucepan.

Clean, wash and dry the mushrooms, cut them in thin slices and wilt them in a little butter in a separate pan. Add the diced venison to the sauteed vegetables and brown rapidly for a few minutes, sprinkling with a glass of red wine. Season with salt and pepper. Turn the heat down, cover and cook for about 1/2 an hour stirring occasionally. Lastly, add the mushrooms.

At this point, cook the pasta in a large pot of boiling salted water. Drain when still "al dente" and add to the sauce. Cook rapidly for a few minutes and serve with the grated parmesan.

Pici al sugo di coniglio
PICI IN RABBIT SAUCE

400 g pici, 1/2 a small rabbit and its liver,
1 medium sized onion, 1 carrot, 1 stalk of celery,
a bunch of parsley, 1 thick slice of streaky bacon,
150 g of minced beef, 1 glass of red wine (scant),
1 tablespoon of tomato preserve, 200 g ripe plum tomatoes,
a little meat stock, salt, pepper.

First prepare the pici following the indications given in the basic recipe (see p. 38).

Then wash, dry and chop the rabbit, putting the liver aside. Chop the onion, carrot, celery, parsley and bacon and sauté them gently in a pot, preferably earthenware.

When they start to turn golden, add the rabbit, minced beef and stew gently, stirring occasionally.

When the meat starts to brown, add the red wine and cook until it evaporates.

Then add the tomato preserve diluted with a little meat stock and cook for a few minutes before adding the washed and chopped tomatoes.

Stir with a wooden spoon, season with salt and pepper and cook over gentle heat for 1 1/2 hours with the lid slightly raised.

After an hour, add the diced liver. Stir occasionally, adding a little meat stock if the sauce is getting too dry.

When the sauce is done, remove the rabbit pieces.

When they are cool, remove the flesh from the bones and put it back into the sauce.

Cook a little longer until the sauce has thickened.

Heat a large pot of water for the pici. Just before it comes to the boil, add some salt. Add the pici. When they are cooked "al dente", drain and pour into a large serv-

ing bowl. Add the boiling sauce. Lastly, sprinkle with a generous helping of grated parmesan (reggiano) and serve very hot.

Risotto verde
GREEN RISOTTO

400 g rice, 200 g beet leaves,
100 g butter,
70 g grated parmesan,
1 l of meat stock,
1 medium-sized onion,
nutmeg, salt.

Clean and wash the beet leaves.
Boil for a few minutes, drain and put through a sieve to obtain a smooth purée.
Melt one tablespoon of butter in a preferably earthenware pot. Stir in the purée with a wooden spoon and leave near the flame.
Melt the remaining butter in a casserole and gently sauté the chopped onion till golden.
Add the rice and sauté it, stirring.
Add some meat stock and season with salt and a pinch of nutmeg. Continue cooking and stirring, gradually adding hot stock. About 5 minutes before the rice is cooked, carefully stir in the beet leaf purée, adding extra stock if necessary. When done, sprinkle with parmesan, stir well and serve very hot.

FISH AND MEAT DISHES

Spezzatino rifinito
VEAL STEW

600 g lean veal muscle, 1 medium sized onion,
1 carrot, 1 stalk of celery, 1 clove of garlic,
a few basil leaves, 1 glass red wine,
350 g ripe tomatoes, 1 cup of stock, extra-virgin olive oil,
salt, pepper.

Cut the muscle into 50g pieces. Peel the onion and garlic. Clean and wash the carrot, stalk of celery and basil leaves. Chop together and sauté in a large pan with abundant oil over gentle heat, stirring with a wooden spoon.

When lightly browned, add the meat and cook for about 10 minutes over a fairly fast flame stirring often. Then sprinkle with the red wine and let it evaporate.

In the meantime, wash and peel the tomatoes and put them through a sieve. Add them to the stew and season with salt and pepper. Cook for 2 1/2 hours over gentle heat, adding meat stock if the stew becomes too dry.

Serve with beans in tomato sauce ("Fagioli all'uccelletto", see recipe p. 106) cooked separately and added to the stew at the last minute.

Lombata di vitello al forno ▶▶

Roasted veal sirloin

*1 kg loin of veal, 50 g bacon, 3 sage leaves,
1 sprig of rosemary, 1 clove of garlic,
extra-virgin olive oil, salt, pepper.*

Finely chop the sage, rosemary and garlic and spread on top of the slices of bacon on a working surface.
Season the loin with salt and pepper. Then place it on top of the bacon.
Wrap the bacon round the loin and tie it firmly with kitchen string. Lightly grease a roasting pan with oil. Put the loin into it and place in the oven at 250°C. After 20 minutes lower, the temperature to 140°C and leave to cook for about an hour.
At this point, turn the oven off but leave the loin inside for another twenty minutes so that the meat cooks inside but remains pink.
Remove the outer covering, cut the roast into fairly thick slices and serve.

Pollo al mattone

Barbecued chicken

*1 young chicken (about 1 kg), 2 cloves of garlic,
1 sprig of sage, hot red pepper, 1/2 glass of extra-virgin olive oil,
salt, pepper.
To garnish: 1 lemon.*

Prepare the chicken for this dish the day before cooking. Clean, wash and dry the chicken. Cut it into 2 parts and flatten with a meat hammer. Put it in a bowl with plenty of oil, the peeled and sliced garlic, sage leaves and marinate in the fridge overnight.

Next morning, remove the chicken from the fridge. Place it skin side down on a grill (preferably over a wood or charcoal fire) and season well with salt, pepper and ground powdered hot red pepper. Place a brick on top and grill it. Take care that there is not too much heat. Then remove the brick, turn the chicken over, brush it with a little oil and cover it with the brick again. Bear in mind that all together it will take about 40 minutes to cook. Serve with lemon quarters and if wished, a side dish of homegrown lettuce.

Polpette
MEAT BALLS

250 g lean beef, 2 fresh sausages, 80 g soft bread, a little milk, 1 small onion, 1 small carrot, a bunch of parsley, 2 eggs, a little flour, a handful of breadcrumbs, nutmeg, extra-virgin olive oil, salt, pepper.

Put the bread in a bowl with a little milk and leave to soak until it's soft.

Meanwhile mince the beef and sausages together. Press the excess moisture out of the bread and add to the meat. Peel the onion. Clean and wash the carrot and parsley. Chop it all together finely. Beat the eggs and add them to the meat seasoning with salt, pepper and nutmeg. At this point, with moist hands, form the meat into oval balls weighing about 60 g each.

Lightly coat them with flour and then with breadcrumbs and put them aside. Heat the oil in a large frying pan. When it is hot, add the meat balls and fry turning them over with a wooden spoon.

When they are done, remove from the frying pan and drain, placing them on absorbent kitchen paper to soak up the excess oil. Lastly, serve with chips and a few lemon segments.

Cappone ripieno arrosto
ROAST STUFFED CAPON

(For 6-8 people) 1 capon (2.5 kg already cleaned),
3 thick slices of bacon fat, 3 pork sausages,
3 cloves of garlic, 1 sprig of sage, 1 tablespoon of butter,
8 pieces of loin of pork, about 1 kg of potatoes,
2-3 bay leaves, 1 l of red wine, 8 rounds of country-style bread
toasted and rubbed with garlic and sprinkled with oil,
1 small glass of cognac, extra-virgin olive oil,
salt, white pepper.

Singe the capon and wash it, first with water and then with red wine. Stuff it with the bacon-fat, sausages, 2 cloves of garlic and sage. Tie it well and season with salt and pepper. Peel and cut the potatoes into chunks. Place the capon in a roasting pan with the loin of pork, potatoes, toasted bread and bay leaves and sprinkle with the wine. Put it in the oven preheated to 200 °C. Turn the capon frequently as it cooks. When done, after about 1 1/2 hours, sprinkle with cognac. When this has evaporated, cut the capon into pieces and serve.

Polpettone
MEAT LOAF

*300 g boiled beef, 2 fresh sausages, 80 g soft bread, 0.5 l of stock,
2 eggs, 1 onion, 1 tablespoon of butter, 40 g parmesan,
3 tablespoons of flour, nutmeg,
2 tablespoons of extra-virgin olive oil, salt, pepper.*

Even if it contains meat, meat loaf is traditionally considered an economical dish, being made of leftovers from boiled beef or stews.
First gind the meat in a foodmill with the sausage and the soft bread, previously damped with stock and squeezed dry. Add the eggs, grated parmesan, salt, pepper, and a pinch of nutmeg and mix well. Shape into a long, rather thick meat-loaf.
Peel and chop the onion. Sauté it gently in the oil and butter in an ovenproof dish. Then add the meatloaf lightly coated with flour. Place the dish in an oven preheated to 160-170 °C and cook the meatloaf, occasionally adding hot stock. After about 30 minutes, remove the meatloaf from the oven.

Leave it to cool well, slice it, arrange the slices on a serving dish and serve, preferably with vegetables sautéed in butter.

Braciole in salsa rossa
VEAL CHOPS IN RED SAUCE

*4 veal chops, 300 g canned tomato pulp, 1 egg, 1 clove of garlic,
a bunch of fresh parsley, ginger, 1 cup of breadcrumbs,
extra-virgin olive oil, salt.*

Beat the eggs with a little salt and immerse the veal chops in them.Chop the garlic, parsley and ginger and sauté in a little oil in a frying pan.
Add the tomatoes, a little water and a pinch of salt and cook over moderate heat with the lid on. Remove the chops from the beaten eggs and coat them with the breadcrumbs. Then fry separately in abundant oil. When done, drain them well and place them in the pan containing the tomato sauce, turn them well to absorb the flavour and serve.

Arrosto di fegatelli
ROAST LIVERS

*650 g pig's liver with its "rete" (o netting),
1 good slice of streaky bacon, a handful of fennel seeds, 2 bay leaves,
1 / 2 glass red wine (scant), 2 tablespoons of wine vinegar,
3-4 tablespoons of extra-virgin olive oil,
salt, pepper.*

Cut the liver into pieces of about 50g each. Wrap each of them in a piece of netting.

Season with salt, pepper and fennel seeds and fix the netting with toothpicks.

Put the pieces of liver in a pan with the oil, the roughly chopped bacon, and the bay leaves.

Cook over a fairly fast flame, stirring occasionally with a wooden spoon and ladling the cooking fat over them.

When they are nearly done, add the wine and vinegar.

Cook until it evaporates. Serve piping hot.

If preferred, the livers can also be cooked on a spit, alternating pieces of liver with cubes of bacon and bread.

Bistecca alla fiorentina ➡➡
FLORENTINE STEAK

2 sirloin beef steaks, extra-virgin olive oil, salt, pepper.
To garnish: 1 lemon.

A good Florentine steak requires top quality meat which has been well aged. It should be about 2.5 cm thick, not having been beaten and weigh about 500 g.

First prepare the charcoal fire. Heat the grill before placing the steaks on top. When one side is cooked, turn them over and season the grilled side with salt and pepper.

Then turn them again to dissolve the salt so that it is evenly distributed and any excess runs off. Remove the steaks from the grill when they are well browned on the outside but still tender and rare on the inside.

Lastly, arrange them on a hot dish and serve with slices of lemon and provide fresh olive oil for everyone to serve themselves.

Ossibuchi alla fiorentina
SHIN OF VEAL FLORENTINE-STYLE

4 slices of shin of veal, 600 g canned tomato pulp, 1 small onion, 1 clove of garlic, 1 bunch of basil, 1 glass of marsala, 1 cup of stock, butter, salt, pepper.

Peel the onion and garlic and chop together with a handful of fresh basil. In a frying pan, heat the butter and gently sauté the vegetables. Then add the shin of veal and brown slowly. Sprinkle with the marsala. When it has evaporated, add the tomato pulp, stock, salt and pepper. Simmer gently. The veal is done when the prongs of a fork sink into the meat easily (1-1/2 hours).

Arrosto misto
MIXED ROAST

4 pork sausages, 4 small pieces of loin of pork, 4 little birds, "Ratta" of pig (membranous netting surrounding pig's abdomen), pieces of stale bread, 2-3 tablespoons of extra-virgin olive oil, bay leaves, salt, pepper.

One by one, wrap the pieces of loin in the netting. Put a piece of bread, 1 sausage, 1 bay leaf, 1 little bird, another bay leaf, a piece of loin and another piece of bread onto skewers. Season with salt and pepper and arrange in a dish. Pour olive oil over them and cook in a hot oven basting frequently with the cooking fat.

Coda di manzo al pomodoro
OXTAILS IN TOMATO SAUCE

*2 oxtails, 500 g bottled tomato pulp, 3 carrots, 1 onion,
1 stalk of celery, 1 clove of garlic, a few leaves of sage,
1 sprig of rosemary, a few leaves of basil, 1 bunch of parsley,
1 cup of stock, extra-virgin olive oil, salt, pepper.*

Finely chop the fresh sage, rosemary, garlic, basil and parsley. In a large pan, sauté this mixture in a little oil until golden and then add the chopped oxtails. Stir and brown the meat and then add the coarsely chopped carrots, celery and onion. Season with salt and pepper. Finally, add the tomato pulp and a little stock. Cover and cook for at least two hours over gentle heat. The oxtails are cooked when the meat comes away from the bone easily.

Baccalà alla livornese
STOCKFISH LIVORNO-STYLE

*500 g stockfish (soaked), 400 g puréed tomatoes,
1 onion, 2 cloves of garlic, 1 tablespoon parsley,
1 cup of flour, extra-virgin olive oil, salt, pepper.*

Remove the bones from the stockfish, cut it into pieces and dry with a cloth. Peel and finely chop the onion with a clove of garlic, then sauté the chopped vegetables in a little oil.

As soon as the onion begins to turn translucent, add the puréed tomatoes.

Cook slowly over moderate heat for about twenty minutes, stirring constantly with a wooden spoon.

Heat a generous quantity of oil in a frying pan together with the remaining garlic.

Lightly flour the pieces of stockfish and fry in the oil as soon as the garlic has browned slightly.

Drain the pieces of fish on paper towels and arrange on a pre-heated serving dish.

Lastly, cover with the tomato sauce and sprinkle with the freshly chopped parsley.

Acciughe fritte ⏩
FRIED ANCHOVIES

500 g fresh anchovies, 2 eggs, 1 small glass of vinegar, 1 cup of flour, extra-virgin olive oil, salt. For the relish: 2 lemons.

Wash the anchovies with water and vinegar, open into two halves, de-scale and rinse, then dry with a teacloth.

Beat the eggs in a bowl with a pinch of salt, dip the anchovies in holding them by the tail, then coat them with flour and place immediately in a pan with sizzling hot oil. Gently brown the fish on both sides, blot off the excess oil rapidly with paper towels and serve immediately, garnished with lemon slices.

Agnello arrosto
ROAST LAMB

1 leg of lamb (about 1 kg), 2 sprigs of rosemary, 3 cloves of garlic,
3 tablespoons of vinegar, 1 glass of extra-virgin olive oil,
salt, pepper.

Mix the oil and vinegar, chop the herbs and garlic and add
to the vinegar and oil, together with a pinch of salt and
freshly ground pepper. Wash and dry the meat. Then marinate in the vinegar and oil emulsion for about 2 hours, turning frequently. When the lamb has absorbed the flavours,
cook in a preheated oven (200 °C) basting with the marinade.
If you desire, when the lamb is half-done, you can add some
peeled and diced potatoes so that they cook in the meat
juices as magnificant accompaniment to the roast.

Buglione di agnello
LAMB STEW

800 g lamb, 2 medium-sized onions, 2 cloves of garlic, hot red pepper,
2 thick slices of streaky bacon, 200 g peeled tomatoes,
1 carrot, 1 l of red wine, 1 / 2 glass wine vinegar (scant),
2 beet leaves, 1 sprig of sage, 1 sprig of rosemary, 1 stalk of celery,
3-4 basil leaves, 1 sprig of calamint, 4 slices of country-style bread,
1 cup of stock, extra-virgin olive oil, salt, pepper.

Cut the lamb into small pieces and marinate for a few
hours or better overnight in red wine with a little wine

vinegar and water, sage, rosemary, celery and basil. Meanwhile, peel and chop one of the onions, one clove of garlic and the hot red pepper.

Heat a little oil, in a preferably earthenware casserole, sauté the chopped vegetables in it, then add the chopped bacon and brown a few more minutes.

After marinating, drain the pieces of lamb. Dry them with a clean cloth and place them in a pan over very gentle heat to remove any excess liquid. Then drain carefully and add to the sautéed mixture, brown them stirring frequently with a wooden spoon. Add the red wine and let it evaporate, cook for a few minutes, then add the peeled and chopped tomatoes, the remaining onion and carrot, cleaned and thinly sliced, and the washed, dried and chopped beet leaves. As the sauce thickens, add a little hot stock. Season with salt, pepper and the calamint and continue to cook gently.

Toast the slices of bread in the oven. Spread them with the remaining clove of garlic finely chopped with a pinch of pepper. Arrange in a large serving dish and cover first with the sauce and then with the lamb pieces. Serve after a few minutes when the bread has soaked up the sauce.

Trippa alla fiorentina
TRIPE FLORENTINE-STYLE

700 g pre-cooked tripe, 400 g peeled tomatoes,
50 g grated parmesan, 2 onions, 2 cloves of garlic,
1 carrot, extra-virgin olive oil, salt, pepper.

Carefully wash the tripe and blanch it for 10 minutes in boiling water. Then rinse it in cold water, dry it and cut it into strips.

Clean and finely chop the onion, carrot and garlic and sauté in a frying pan with a little oil. When the onion is tender, add the tripe and after a few minutes the peeled and chopped tomato. Season with salt and pepper, cover and cook until on tasting, the tripe melts in your mouth.

If when the tripe is nearly done, the sauce is too liquid, let it simmer without the lid, until it thickens. Lastly, stir in the grated parmesan, mix well and serve. This simple, homemade version of Florentine tripe, the most traditional tripe recipe, can be enriched by the addition of other herbs and spices such as celery, parsley, rosemary, basil, marjoram, cloves and even nutmeg to the original sautéed onion.

Polpette di trippa
TRIPE BALLS

400 g pre-cooked tripe, 250 g puréed tomatoes, 50 g cured ham, the soft inside of 2 bread rolls, 30 g grated parmesan, 2 eggs, 1 bunch of parsley, 1 onion, 1 carrot, 2 cloves of garlic, 3 leaves of basil, 1 cup of flour, 2 tablespoons of milk, extra-virgin olive oil, nutmeg, salt, pepper.

Wash the tripe and blanch in boiling water. Grind it in a meat grinder together with the ham.

Put it in a bowl and add the bread softened in milk, squeezed dry and crumbled, the eggs, grated parmesan, chopped parsley and basil, salt, pepper and a pinch of nutmeg. Stir carefully to incorporate all the ingredients, then mould the mixture into little balls. Lightly coat with flour and deep-fry in hot oil.

When the meatballs are done, dry them on paper towels. Then sauté the finely chopped garlic, carrot, and onion in a little oil in a wide pan.

When the vegetables are soft, add the meatballs and the puréed tomatoes.

Cover and cook gently for about an hour.

Insalata di trippa
TRIPE SALAD

600 g pre-cooked tripe,
200 g dried "cannellini" beans,
200 g spring onions, 200 g potatoes,
1 celery heart,
salt, pepper, baking soda.

Tripe is a great Tuscan passion and there are a thousand different, original ways of preparing it.

A connoisseur's delight, this recipe can be served cold as a substantial snack or as a summer dish.

The day before cooking, put the beans to soak overnight. The next day, drain them and boil them with a pinch of baking soda.

Boil the potatoes separately; drain and leave to cool.
Wash the tripe and cook it in boiling water for 10 minutes.
Then cut it into strips. Finely slice the onions and celery
and dice the cooked, peeled potatoes.
Add all the ingredients to the tripe and season with plenty
of oil, salt, and freshly ground white pepper.
Carefully stir and serve when fully cooled.

Arista ⏩
ROAST SADDLE OF PORK

*1 kg boned saddle of pork, 2 cloves of garlic, sprigs of rosemary,
extra-virgin olive oil, salt, whole black pepper.*

Peel and chop the garlic. Mix with salt and abundant freshly ground pepper.
Then make incisions in the meat and stuff with the fresh
garlic mixture.
Tie it with kitchen twine. Slip the rosemary, cut into short
pieces, under the twine. Season the roast lightly with salt and
pepper. Place it in a roasting tin well greased with olive oil
and cook in a moderate oven (170-180 °C) for about 1 hour.
When it is nearly done, turn up the oven to brown the roast
well. Remove from the oven, untie and let the roast cool a
little before slicing it. Place the slices on a serving dish and
baste them with the cooking juices.
In general, it is better to use a rather large piece of meat for
this recipe. However, roast saddle of pork keeps very well
in the fridge for a few days.

Canocchie alla viareggina
SQUILL FISH VIAREGGIO-STYLE

2 kg squill fish, 2 cloves of garlic, hot red pepper,
1 cup of tomato sauce, extra-virgin olive oil,
slices of country-style bread, salt, pepper.

Wash and dry the squill fish carefully, and sauté in a pan with a little oil and with the peeled crushed garlic. Add the tomato sauce, the hot red pepper and, if necessary, a tablespoon of water. Season with salt and pepper and cook over moderate heat for half an hour.
Finally, serve the fish on slices of toasted bread, after basting with the cooking juices.

Pollo in fricassea
CHICKEN FRICASSÉE

1 young chicken (about 1 kg),
1 medium sized onion, 1 carrot, 1 stalk of celery,
1 tablespoon of butter, 250 ml stock, 1 bunch of parsley,
1 tablespoon of flour, 2 egg yolks, 1 lemon,
4 tablespoons of extra-virgin olive oil,
salt, pepper.

Wash the chicken, dry it and cut it into pieces.
Clean, wash and dry the carrot, stalk of celery and parsley and tie them in a little bundle together with the sliced onion. Heat the oil and butter in a pan, preferably earthenware. Add

a tablespoon of flour and stir carefully with a wooden spoon. When the roux starts to brown, add a little meat stock and stir. When it starts to boil, add the bundle of vegetables and cook over medium heat for a few minutes. Then add the chicken, salt and pepper. Cover and cook for about 1/2 an hour, stirring occasionally. If the sauce becomes too dry, add a little more stock.

Meanwhile beat the egg yolks in a bowl with the lemon juice. When the chicken is done, remove the bundle of vegetables.

Take the pot off the heat and pour the egg yolk mixture onto the chicken, stirring vigorously to obtain a smooth sauce.

Gallinella alle olive
YOUNG HEN WITH OLIVES

1 young hen (about 1.2 kg),
1 medium-sized onion, 1 carrot, 1 stalk of celery,
1 glass of red wine, 1 cup of stock,
200 g green olives in brine, 200 g spring onions,
1/2 glass of extra-virgin olive oil, salt, pepper.

Clean the hen, removing the entrails. Wash, dry and cut into 8 pieces.

Heat the oil in an earthenware pot. Peel the onion, clean and wash the carrot and the celery. Chop the vegetables, add to the oil and sauté over gentle heat. Add the pieces of hen, browning on all sides, then sprinkle with the red wine.

If necessary, add a ladleful of meat stock. Season with salt and pepper and cook over medium heat. Meanwhile peel and blanch the spring onions in boiling water. Then drain and set aside.

When the hen is done, remove it from the pan.

Rub the juices and vegetables through a sieve and return to the pan, adding the pieces of hen.

Then wash the olives and add them, along with the spring onions, to the sauce.

If necessary, add a litle stock. Cook until the sauce has thickened. Serve hot.

Scottiglia ▶▶
MEAT STEW

1 kg of mixed meats (guinea-fowl, chicken, rabbit,
pigeon, veal, pork), 1 onion, 1 carrot, 1 stalk of celery,
500 g fresh tomatoes, 2 cloves of garlic, 1 hot red pepper,
1 bunch of parsley, 2 lemons, 1 glass of red wine,
250 ml of meat stock, 6 slices of country-style bread,
extra-virgin olive oil, salt.

Scottiglia, also called "Cacciucco di carni", is a typical Tuscan recipe, a perfect supper for a happy group of friends.

The quantities suggested here are considered for a party of 15 people.

First clean the fowls, wash and dry and cut into pieces. Cut the lean pork and veal into pieces. Peel a clove of garlic and the onion, clean and wash the celery, carrot and parsley. Chop them fine with the hot red pepper and sauté in a large pot,

preferably earthenware, in 3-4 tablespoons of hot oil. When the vegetables are golden, add the meat and brown over a fairly fast flame, turning with a wooden spoon. Add the lemon juice, let it evaporate and add the red wine. Cook over moderate heat until the sauce has thickened considerably. Then add the tomatoes (peeled after having been briefly plunged in boiling water to loosen the skins) and a little stock. Season with salt and continue to cook, stirring occasionally. When the stew is done, there should be quite a lot of thinnish sauce. Toast the slices of bread in the oven and rub them with the remaining clove of garlic. Place them in the soup bowls, cover with the pieces of meat and the sauce. Leave to rest for a few minutes and then serve.

Pollo fritto alla toscana
FRIED CHICKEN TUSCAN-STYLE

*1 chicken (about 1.2 kg), 250 g flour, 5 eggs,
extra-virgin olive oil, salt.*

Carefully clean the chicken and remove the bones. Cut in pieces. In a bowl, beat the eggs with a pinch of salt and 1 tablespoon of oil.
Then add the flour a little at a time, mixing continuously, to form a thick, smooth batter. Coat the chicken pieces in the batter and deep fry in hot oil. When browned, drain and dry on absorbent paper towels before placing on a serving dish. This recipe can be prepared using chicken breasts alone.

Galantina di pollo
CHICKEN IN ASPIC

(For 6-8 people)
1 chicken (about 1.8 kg),
100 g cooked ham, 100 g bacon fat,
100 g corned tongue, 40 pistachios,
1 kg stuffing made up of lean pork
and veal and the meat from chicken legs,
1 dl dry marsala, 1 small glass of cognac,
50 g grated parmesan, 2 eggs,
40 g black truffles, 2-3 sheets of isinglass (gelatine),
spices, nutmeg, salt, pepper.

This recipe requires a bit of time and effort. It is advisable to prepare the chicken 24 hours before cooking, because, leaving it to rest in the fridge overnight, you can obtain the best results.

It is served cut into slices like a sausage, and can be eaten as a starter or a main course. The quantities indicated here are sufficient for 6-8 people.

First prepare the chicken, removing the skin and bones. Cut the breast into strips. Marinate with the coarsely chopped ham, tongue, bacon fat and diced truffle in the cognac and marsala. Season with salt and pepper and a pinch of nutmeg. Leave in a cool place for about 1/2 an hour.

In the meantime, prepare the stuffing by mincing the meat from the chicken legs, the lean veal and pork.

Season with salt and pepper and add a pinch of nutmeg, the grated parmesan and the eggs. Blend carefully.

Put through a vegetable mill, then add the skinned pistachios. Lay the chicken skin out carefully on a clean, slightly damp cloth. Spread a good helping of stuffing and pieces of marinated meat on top.

Then cover with the remaining stuffing.

Wrap the skin round the galantine, sew it up with a needle and thread and weigh.

Wrap the cloth round it sufficiently tightly and tie with a string. Place in a large pot of water when this has reached the boiling point. Add the chicken carcass, herbs, salt and isinglass and simmer until done.

It needs 35 minutes cooking time per kilo.

When it is done, drain, leave to cool and tighten the string. Lastly, put the galantine in the fridge with a weight on top. Serve it the next day, cut in slices decorated with gelatine. Instead of chicken, you can use a capon.

Faraona alla creta
GUINEA-FOWL BAKED IN A CLAY MOULD

1 guinea-fowl (1.5 kg) already hung,
4 slices of fatty bacon, 1 sprig of sage,
1 sprig of rosemary, 4 juniper berries,
4 tablespoons of extra-virgin olive oil,
salt, pepper.

This fascinating recipe, in which the guinea-fowl is baked in a clay mould, can also be used for other birds: pheasant, pigeon or chicken. First clean, wash and dry the guinea-fowl. Season the body cavity with salt, pepper, rosemary, sage and juniper berries. Bard it with slices of bacon. Then wrap it in well-greased oily paper. Next, encase it in a sheet of dampened yellow oven paper. Wet the clay (the best kind ist the grey clay used to make terracotta tiles) and flatten it with your hands.

Place the bird in the middle and wrap the clay around it, moulding it into the shape of the bird. Seal it hermetically. Then place it in the oven at 180 °C and bake for 3 hours until the clay has dried and a few cracks start to appear. Break the mould in front of your guests using a small hammer. Take care to remove all the clay fragments and serve.

Uccelletti con crostini
SMALL BIRDS WITH CROÛTONS

4 small birds,
8 pieces of country-style bread weighing 20 g each,
2 sausages, 8 bay leaves,
8 small pieces of pork sirloin weighing about 20 g each,
netting formed of the membrane surrounding a pig's abdomen,
1/2 small glass of extra-virgin olive oil,
salt, pepper.

Clean the small birds carefully, flame them, remove the entrails, wash and dry.
Cut the sausages and pork sirloin in half, then wrap in pig's abdomen netting.
On the spitfork place a piece of bread, 1/2 sausage, a bay-

leaf, a bird, another bayleaf, a piece of pork sirloin, another piece of bread, and so on, until having used all the prepared ingredients.

Season with salt and pepper and set the spitfork on the turnspit, brush with oil and remove from heat only when the meat is golden and crispy.

If you don't have a spit, you can also cook the small birds in a normal oven: in this case use 4 long meat skewers. Prepare them as described above.

Then arrange them on an oven tray with a little oil; bake in a hot oven after having sprinkled with a bit of wine.

Pollo alla diavola   ⏩
DEVILED CHICKEN

1 chicken (about 1.2 kg), hot red pepper,
1 cup of extra-virgin olive oil, salt, pepper.
To garnish: 1 lemon.

Clean the chicken and cut it in half. Then flatten it with a meat hammer on a wooden cutting board, taking care not to break the bones.

In a bowl, prepare a sauce by emulsifying the oil with the lemon juice, salt, pepper and a good pinch of hot red pepper. Marinate the chicken in this sauce for about 1/2 an hour, turning it frequently. Cook the chicken over a barbecue, or if this is not possible under the oven grill.

After about 40 minutes serve the chicken garnished with slices of lemon and, if you like, with a side dish of salad greens.

Fagiano tartufato
Truffled pheasant

1 pheasant (about 1.2 kg) already hung,
150 g cured ham with its fat in a single slice,
150 g bacon, 150 g black truffles,
1/2 glass cognac, 1 glass dry white wine,
1 sprig sage, 250 ml cream,
extra-virgin olive oil, salt, pepper.

The day before cooking the pheasant, prepare the stuffing. Clean the truffles thoroughly, chop them (leaving some flakes for decoration), mix them with the chopped ham and amalgamate with a little cognac.

Stuff the pheasant with this mixture and place it in the refrigerator for a few hours to absorb the fragrance of the truffles. Prior to cooking, wrap the bird in the slices of bacon, inserting a few leaves of sage, and tie it well with kitchen twine. Season with salt and pepper and place in a pan, preferably earthenware, with a little oil.

Cover and brown over direct heat for a few minutes, then place the pan, still covered, in the oven at 200 °C. Cook for about 20 minutes, then remove the cover and moisten the bird with the white wine.

Let the wine evaporate, then baste with the melted fat and continue cooking at a low temperature.

When the pheasant is done, remove it from oven, cut it in pieces and reserve the stuffing.

Add the rest of the cognac to the gravy that is left in the pan, skim off the excess fat, then add the pheasant stuffing and the cream and boil for a few minutes.

Arrange the pieces of pheasant in a pyrex dish, pour over them the gravy mixed with the stuffing, and garnish with truffle flakes. Serve piping hot.

Tordi in salsa
THRUSHES IN SAUCE

*8 thrushes, 80 g cured ham, 80 g streaky bacon, 1 carrot,
1 medium-sized onion, 1 stalk of celery, a few juniper berries,
50 g butter, 1/2 glass white wine, meat stock,
3-4 tablespoons extra-virgin olive oil, salt, pepper.*

Clean the thrushes carefully, wash and dry with a clean cloth. Clean and wash the celery and carrot, peel the onion and finely chop together with the ham and streaky bacon. Brown the chopped vegetables over moderate heat in a frying pan with the oil and a knob of butter.

Place the thrushes in the browned vegetables, add salt and a dust of pepper, and garnish the interior of the birds with the juniper berries. Sauté a little more, pour in the white wine and let it evaporate, then add a little stock. Cook over slow heat for 1 hour, until the sauce has reduced and thickened.

Meanwhile prepare the croûtons with country-style bread. Melt a knob of butter in a flat pan, arrange the slices of bread in the pan and sauté on both sides. Serve the thrushes with the piping hot croûtons.

Piccioni in arrosto morto
PIGEONS IN A CASSEROLE

4 young pigeons, 1 onion, 80 g bacon fat, 1 clove of garlic,
2 sausages, 1 glass of red wine, 1 cup of stock,
extra-virgin olive oil, salt, pepper.

Flame the pigeons, clean and remove entrails; wash and dry
the birds. Peel the onion and chop half of it together with
the bacon fat, sausages, salt and pepper. Fill the gullet of each
pigeon with the chopped mixture and then place the birds
in a casserole, preferably earthenware, with a little oil and
a finely chopped blend of the remaining garlic and onion.
Cook over low heat adding a little stock now and then;
when the pigeons are nearly done, add a little red wine and
allow to evaporate. Serve the pigeons piping hot.

Lepre in salmì
HARE IN SALMÌ

(For 8 people) 1 hare (about 2 kg),
1 l red wine, 300 g of mushrooms, 20 g bacon in a single slab,
30 small onions, 1 stalk of celery, 1 carrot, 1 onion,
1 clove of garlic, a few sage leaves, 1 sprig of rosemary,
1 small glass of brandy, 100 g butter, 50 g flour,
1 dl hare's blood, 1 dl cream, salt.

Clean the hare (reserving 1 dl of the blood) and cut it in
pieces. In a bowl prepare the marinade with the wine, the

cleaned and coarsely chopped celery, carrot and onion, the crushed garlic and the sage and rosemary leaves. Place the pieces of hare in the marinade and leave them for 48 hours. Then drain the meat, dry it and sauté in a casserole with a tablespoon of sizzling butter. When well browned, dredge with flour, flame with brandy, add the marinade and season with salt, then continue cooking at medium heat for about two hours.

Meanwhile dice the bacon, blanch it and brown it in a frying pan. Clean the onions and sauté in a little butter. Clean the mushrooms and rinse briefly under running water, dry, slice and sauté in the remaining butter. Add the vegetables to the hare and cook for another 15 minutes.

Shortly before removing from heat, add the cream mixed with the reserved hare's blood; simmer for a few minutes, and serve.

Cinghiale stufato
WILD BOAR STEW

*800 g wild boar sirloin, 2 cloves of garlic, 1 onion,
1 carrot, 1 stalk of celery, 1 spice clove,
1 pinch of cinnamon, 1/2 cup of flour, 1 bay leaf, 1 sprig of
rosemary, 1 l red wine, 80 g of fresh tomatoes,
extra-virgin olive oil, salt, pepper.*

The day before cooking, pour the red wine into a basin and add the cleaned and sliced carrot, onion and celery, a peeled crushed clove of garlic, the spice clove, bay leaf and cinnamon. Place the wild boar sirloin in this marinade and leave to marinate for 24 hours in a cool spot. After this time, drain the meat and cut in pieces.

Peel the remaining clove of garlic, slice it and lightly brown it with a little oil in a pan, preferably earthenware. Add the lightly floured wild boar.

Season with salt, pepper and rosemary and brown well. Then add the peeled tomatoes and begin to pour in the marinade. Cover with a lid and simmer at moderate heat for about 2 hours (or until the meat is tender), stirring occasionally and adding more of the marinade if it is too dry.

Serve piping hot.

Polenta con le aringhe
POLENTA WITH HERRINGS

300 g of cornmeal, 4 smoked herrings, 300 g grated pecorino cheese, 200 g sliced bacon fat, vinegar, extra-virgin olive oil, salt.

Prepare the polenta by pouring the corn meal into one litre of boiling salted water. Mix well, bring back to boil, and simmer for half an hour, stirring continously. Then brown the slices of bacon fat in a griddle pan and add to the polenta, continuing to stir well to avoid any lumpiness. Cook for another 10-15 minutes, then pour out onto a cutting board. Meanwhile wash the herrings to remove excess salt, and boil them lightly. Cut them into small pieces and dress with oil and vinegar. Slice the polenta, place a piece of herring on each slice and dust with grated pecorino cheese. If preferred, lightly broil each piece prepared as above before serving.

Tegamaccio
FISH HOTCH-POTCH

1 kg of mixed fish composed of pike, tench and eel,
1 onion, 2 cloves of garlic, 1 glass of red wine (scant), 200 g fresh
peeled tomatoes (or 80 g tomato preserves),
2-3 basil leaves, 2 hot red peppers,
4 slices country-style bread, extra-virgin olive oil, salt.

Fish hotch-potch is the most widely known speciality of the area round Lake Chiusi. It is a sort of freshwater fish soup, which should be prepared using at least two different types of fish. Its taste is further enhanced if it contains an abundant presence of eel.

After cleaning the fish and removing the entrails, wash it and cut it into pieces. Peel the onion and a clove of garlic, finely chop and sauté with a little oil in an earthenware pot, over moderate heat. Place the fish pieces in the browned vegetables and gently brown for a few minutes, then add the wine and allow to evaporate. Add salt and the hot red pepper. After a few minutes, add the basil leaves and the tomatoes passed through the vegetable mill (or tomato preserves diluted with a little hot water). Bring to the boil and simmer for about two hours, so that the sauce reduces, then remove from heat. Take out the large fish bones, remove all flesh from the heads and return the body and flesh to the pan. Meanwhile, toast the slices of bread in the oven, rub them with the remaining clove of garlic and place them in the pot to soak up the sauce. Serve immediately in the same pot, or if you prefer, in individual bowls, placing a slice of toasted bread on the bottom of each bowl.

Piccioni ripieni
STUFFED PIGEONS

4 young pigeons, 2 sausages, 2 eggs, 1 glass of milk,
100 g of lean veal, soft bread from inside 2-3 rolls, 1 small onion,
40 g of grated parmesan, 1 pinch of marjoram or calamint,
extra-virgin olive oil, nutmeg, salt, pepper.

Flame the pigeons, then remove the entrails, setting them aside; wash the birds and dry with a cloth. Meanwhile soak the bread with milk in a basin.

Clean and wash the pigeon giblets, allow to drain and then chop them together with the sausage and lean veal. Squeeze out the softened bread and add to the chopped ingredients, then work in the eggs, salt, pepper, a pinch of nutmeg and the grated parmesan.

Stuff the pigeons with this mixture. Season them with salt and pepper and arrange in a pan with the oil and butter, the peeled and chopped onion, a pinch of calamint or marjoram. Cover and cook over low heat for about 1 hour, stirring occasionally with a wooden spoon. If necessary, add a little meat stock. Serve the pigeons piping hot.

Tonno ubriaco alla livornese
DRUNKEN TUNA LIVORNO-STYLE

4 slices of tuna weighing roughly 100 g each, 1 onion,
1 clove of garlic, 1 tablespoon chopped parsley, 1 glass red wine,
flour, extra-virgin olive oil, salt, pepper.

Sauté the finely chopped onion with the peeled and crushed garlic. Lightly flour the slices of tuna. When the onion has become completely translucent, remove the garlic and place the slices of tuna in the pan. Season with salt and pepper and sprinkle with parsley. Brown the tuna before drenching it in wine, from hence the name "drunken". Return to moderate heat for another 10 minutes, reducing the juices to a creamy, flavourful sauce.

Brustico
BARBECUED FISH

800 g of mixed freshwater fish (pike, tench, eel or perch),
a few sage leaves, 1 sprig of rosemary, calamint, garlic,
extra-virgin olive oil, salt, pepper.

'Brustico' is a traditional dish prepared in the vicinity of the Lake of Chiusi, and it is sometimes mischievously called

"Porsenna Piss" by impish souls of the Lake of Trasimeno. In the past it was always prepared on the glowing embers of a reed bonfire that fishermen would build on the shores of the lake. The lake used to abound in fish and bonfires were thus a frequent and picturesque sight.

To prepare this recipe, the procedure is as follows: clean the fish, removing the entrails, and wash them. Then build a fire and broil the fish over it, traditionally speared on a stick of laurel wood, until it is slightly burned on the outside. Remove the fish from the fire, detach the burnt skin and place on a serving dish. Season with salt and pepper, crushed garlic, sage, rosemary and calamint, then dribble with olive oil.

Triglie alla livornese
MULLET LIVORNO-STYLE

8 fairly large mullets, 500 g puréed tomatoes, 1/2 onion,
2 cloves of garlic, 1/2 bay leaf, 1 tablespoon chopped parsley,
1 sprig of thyme, 1/2 cup of flour, extra-virgin olive oil, salt, pepper.

Prepare a very finely chopped mix of onion and garlic together with the crushed chopped thyme.

Then gently brown the vegetables in oil until the onion is translucent. Add the puréed tomatoes and cook over moderate heat for about twenty minutes, stirring occasionally with a wooden spoon.

Meanwhile clean the fish, then wash, dry and coat them in flour. Brown them lightly in a frying pan with a little oil, flavoured with the remaining crushed clove of garlic. When

the fish are well browned, drain them and place them in the pan with the tomato sauce. Add pepper; cook for another ten minutes, occasionally turning the fish gently in the pan without breaking them. Serve garnished with finely chopped parsley.

Cinghiale in agrodolce
SWEET AND SOUR WILD BOAR

800 g boned shoulder of wild boar, 1 small onion,
40 g streaky bacon, 40 g butter, 1 tablespoon of flour, 40 g sugar,
2 cloves of garlic, 1 / 2 glass of vinegar, 1 cup of stock, 1 bay leaf,
40 g bitter chocolate, 30 g sultanas, 30 g pine nuts,
20 g candied citron and orange, 2 dried plums,
4 cherries preserved in alcohol, salt, pepper.
For the marinade: 1 medium-sized onion, 1 carrot,
1 stalk of celery, 1 clove of garlic, 1 bunch of parsley,
a few sprigs of thyme, a few bay leaves, 1 l of dry white wine,
1 glass of red wine vinegar, a few cloves, extra-virgin olive oil,
whole black pepper. For garnishing: cherries preserved in alcohol.

Start to marinate the wild boar meat 3 days before cooking. Prepare the marinade by browning the finely chopped onion, carrot, celery, garlic, parsley, thyme and the bay leaves in an earthenware pot. When they are golden brown, add the vinegar and 3-4 glasses of dry white wine, a few spice cloves and some peppercorns. Boil for a few minutes, then let cool. Meanwhile tie the shoulder of wild boar as if preparing a roast, place it in a basin and pour over it the cooled marinade. If the meat is not entirely covered, add additional white wine. Cover and leave to marinate in the fridge for 3 days. After this time, drain the meat (reserving the marinade), dry with a clean kitchen cloth and season with salt, pepper and a finely chopped clove of garlic. Then chop the streaky bacon with the remaining onion and brown in a little oil in a large pan. Add the joint of wild boar. Brown evenly, then add the marinade, a little at a time. If the liquid is insufficient, add a little meat stock and more white wine. Simmer for 2 hours over low heat. Then remove the meat from the cooking juices and set it aside. Strain the juices, add the butter which has been cut into the flour, and mix, carefully smoothing out any lumps. Prepare the sweet-and-sour sauce. Heat the sugar in an earthenware pot together with a clove of crushed garlic, a chopped bay leaf and the vinegar. Mix, and when the sugar has dissolved, add the grated bitter chocolate. When the chocolate has melted, add the chopped pine nuts, the washed, soaked and drained sultanas, the diced candied citron and orange, the plums and the alcohol-preserved cherries, chopped after removing the pips. Add to the mixture the sauce prepared as described above and mix well. Cut the wild boar in pieces, place in a pyrex dish, warm briefly over moderate heat and pour on the sweet-and-sour sauce. Serve piping hot at table, garnished with some of the alcohol-preserved cherries.

Lesso rifatto
TWICE-COOKED BOILED MEAT

500 g leftover boiled meat, 1 onion, 300 g ripe tomatoes, a few leaves of fresh basil, 4 tablespoons of extra-virgin olive oil, salt, pepper.

This recipe, also known as "stiracchio", does not require much effort or time. Chop the boiled meat into slices. Wash the tomatoes, remove their seeds and chop into tiny pieces. Peel and chop the onion and sauté in a little oil over medium heat.

When lightly browned, add the meat, tomatoes, basil, salt and pepper. Cover and cook for about 10 minutes over low heat. When done, arrange the slices of meat on a serving dish and pour the sauce over them.

Agnello alle olive   ▶▶
LAMB WITH OLIVES

*1 kg lamb, 250 g puréed tomatoes, 150 g pitted black olives,
4 cloves of garlic, 1 glass of dry white wine, 1 lemon,
1 sprig of rosemary, 1 tablespoon of vinegar, 1 cup of stock, extra-
virgin olive oil, salt, pepper.*

Different parts of lamb can be used for this dish, such as pieces of shoulder, neck, ribs, breast etc. Wash and dry the pieces of meat before gently sautéing in a little oil and vinegar to get rid of some of the fat. Drain and transfer to a large pan in which you have previously sautéed the garlic and rosemary in a little oil. Season with salt and pepper and add the wine. When it has evaporated, remove the meat from the pan, keeping it warm. Add the puréed tomato and chopped olives. Cook for a few moments; add the pieces of lamb. Cook over low heat for about 1 hour, adding a little stock if necessary. Serve boiling hot, preferably with slices of toasted polenta.

EGGS AND SIDE DISHES

Fagioli al fiasco
BEANS IN A BOTTLE

350 g shelled "canellini" beans,
2 cloves of garlic, 1/2 glass extra-virgin olive oil,
6 sage leaves, salt, pepper.

This recipe is an ancient tradition that calls for time and patience. First, take a two-litre wide-neck glass flask, remove the straw casing and wash carefully.

Fill it 2/3 full of beans, then add the oil and the coarsely chopped sage, crushed garlic and about two glasses of water. Stop up the bottle with the straw casing, or use tow, oakum or cotton, but without pressing down too hard, so that the steam can escape during the cooking process.

At this point the Tuscan farmers used to place the flask upright on the glowing embers covered with warm ashes, allowing the beans to cook for at least 5 hours or even overnight.

In the lack of a fireplace, you can place the flask in the oven at moderate heat, in a pyrex dish half filled with water. The beans are done when all the water in the flask has evaporated and the oil has been completely absorbed. Take the beans out of the bottle, add salt and lots of pepper and drench them with extra-virgin olive oil.

Carciofi ripieni
STUFFED ARTICHOKES

4 large artichokes (8 if small), 1 lemon,
1 egg, 20 g dried mushrooms, 80 g chicken livers,
1 sausage, 50 g streaky bacon, 1/2 cup soft bread,
1 bunch parsley, 1 small onion, 1/2 cup of stock,
1 glass dry white wine, 1 tablespoon butter,
extra-virgin olive oil, salt, white pepper.

Clean and wash the artichokes, remove the tough outer leaves, and place in a pot of boiling water soured with lemon juice. Blanch the artichokes briefly and drain as soon as the water comes back to the boil. Allow to cool.

Meanwhile wash the dried mushrooms and soak them in a little warm water. Soak the bread in a little stock, then squeeze it dry. When the artichokes have cooled, remove the stalk, scoop out their insides with a sharp knife, and chop the insides together with the stalk in a bowl.

Squeeze dry and chop the mushrooms. Chop the chicken livers, crumble the sausage and the squeezed soft bread, and add these ingredients to the bowl containing the finely chopped onion, parsley and streaky bacon. Lastly, add the egg yolk, season with salt and pepper and mix well.

Fill the artichokes with this mixture. Place them in a deep pan with abundant oil, flake them with butter and dust with white pepper.

Cover, and bake in a moderate oven for 30 minutes. Then sprinkle the artichokes with the white wine and continue to cook covered for another 1/2 hour.

Fagioli all'uccelletto
BEANS IN TOMATO SAUCE

500 g shelled fresh "cannellini" beans, 2 cloves of garlic, 3-4 sage leaves, 150ml of puréed tomatoes, extra-virgin olive oil, salt, pepper.

Pour the beans into an earthenware pot and cover with cold, lightly salted water. Place the pot over heat, bring rapidly to the boil, cover and reduce heat to barely perceptible simmering for 1 hour, then drain. In a saucepan, heat a little oil and sauté the garlic and sage, then add the beans, still warm. Stir and cook for 5 minutes. Add the puréed tomatoes, salt and pepper and cook uncovered for about 15 minutes.
"Fagioli all'uccelletto" is a highly flexible recipe, since it can serve as side dish to a wide variety of main dishes, but can also be used as a main dish in its own right.

Zucchine al funghetto
COURGETTES WITH MUSHROOMS

550 g courgettes, 200 g peeled fresh tomatoes, 1 onion, 1 carrot, 1 clove garlic, 150 gr fresh mushrooms and 20 g dried mushrooms, extra-virgin olive oil, salt, pepper.

Trim, wash and dry the courgettes, and cut into fairly small pieces. Prepare the mushrooms: if you have fresh mushrooms, clean and wash them under running water, dry with a freshly laundered teacloth, and cut into slices. If you are using dried mushrooms, soak them in a small amount of water, then squeeze them out carefully and chop lightly. Then peel the onion and finely chop together with the carrot and the clove of garlic; sauté this mixture for a few minutes in a shallow pan, preferably earthenware, with a little oil. Add the courgettes and allow the cooking juices to reduce before adding the peeled tomatoes that have been rubbed through the sieve or vegetable mill, and the sliced or chopped mushrooms. Season with salt and pepper, and return to heat until the sauce has reduced and thickened. Serve hot.

Ciancinfricola

8 eggs, 1 clove of garlic, 1 small onion, 2 ripe tomatoes,
1 / 2 cup of stock, extra-virgin oilve oil, salt, pepper.

"Ciancinfricola" (or rather, "ciancinfri'ola") is a word deriving from dialect verbs "cianciare" and "sfricolare", and it conveys a very good idea of what goes on in the midst of a general 'cook-up', where the recipe calls for everything to be mixed and thrown in together. Peel the garlic and onion, chop and sauté gently with a little oil in a pot, preferably earthenware, stirring with a wooden spoon, then add the well washed and chopped tomatoes (peeled after having briefly plunged them into boiling water to loosen the skins) as well as a tablespoon of stock. Season with salt and pepper, and cook over low heat until the tomato is almost entirely dry.

Meanwhile beat the eggs in a bowl and then pour into the pot with the reduced tomato sauce; mix vigorously and cook until the eggs have absorbed all the sauce.

Frittata al tartufo
OMELETTE WITH TRUFFLES

8 eggs, 1 small black truffle, 2 tablespoons grated parmesan, extra-virgin olive oil, salt, pepper.

Brush the truffle and grate half of it. Beat the eggs in a bowl, add the parmesan and the grated truffle, season with salt and pepper. Then heat a little oil in a shallow pan and pour the eggs in, allowing the omelet to cook without turning or flipping, so that it remains creamy on the surface. When it is done, slide it delicately onto the warmed serving dish, being careful not to overturn it. Lastly, dust it with the remaining portion of the truffle, sliced with a truffel-slicer.

Zucchine ripiene
STUFFED COURGETTES

8 medium-sized courgettes, 250 g boiled meat,
70 g soft bread, a tablespoon of butter,
2 eggs, 1 glass of milk, 30 g grated parmesan,
nutmeg, salt, pepper.

Stuffed courgettes are often prepared when there is a certain

quantity of boiled beef available. Clean and wash the courgettes, cut into halves, scoop out the flesh and reserve. Blanch the courgette halves in boiling water, drain and lay out on a clean cloth to dry. Meanwhile, put the bread in a basin with a little milk and leave to soften. Chop the boiled beef, add the eggs, grated parmesan, salt, pepper, a pinch of nutmeg, the reserved courgette flesh, the squeezed and crumbled bread and mix well. Then pass the mixture through a food mill and stuff the scooped-out courgettes with it. Place them in a pan greased with butter and bake in the oven at 170-180 °C for about 30 minutes. When the courgettes have turned golden brown, serve them hot.

Frittata in trippa
OMELETTE IN TRIPE

8 eggs, 250 g puréed tomatoes, 1 onion,
grated parmesan,
1 tablespoon chopped parsley, butter,
extra-virgin olive oil, salt, pepper.
To complete the presentation: grated parmesan.

Beat the eggs together with 2 tablespoons of parmesan, the parsley and a pinch of salt, then prepare a number of thin pancake-type omelettes using a small frying pan greased with butter. Set aside. Meanwhile, after peeling and finely slicing the onion, wilt it in a wide pan with a little heated oil. As soon as the onion softens, pour the puréed tomatoes into the frying pan and cook slowly for 15 minutes. Roll up the pancakes on a wooden board and slice as if they were tagliatelle of pasta. Put them back in the tomato sauce for another 15 minutes, to absorb the flavour. Serve with a dusting of grated parmesan.

Funghi ripieni
STUFFED MUSHROOMS

13 medium-sized cep mushrooms, 1 onion, 1 egg,
2 cloves of garlic, 50 g parmesan, 100 g lean ground meat,
soft part of 1 bread roll, 1 tablespoon chopped parsley, breadcrubs,
extra-virgin olive oil, salt, pepper.

Clean the mushrooms and reserve one, to be used for the stuffing. Remove the stalks and place 12 mushroom caps in a hot oven for 5 minutes, in order to dry them a little. Chop the reserved mushroom together with all the stems. Prepare a chopped vegetable mixture using the peeled and finely sliced onion and garlic; as soon as they become translucent, add the ground meat. Mix and brown the meat before adding the chopped mushroom and parsley. Then remove from heat and incorporate the egg-yolk and soft bread (softened with a drop of water and squeezed well). Mix to obtain a paste; then stuff it into the mushroom caps. Dust the mushrooms with breadcrumbs and place them in a hot oven for 20 minutes. Brown the breadcrumbs until they have a golden gratiné topping. Serve hot from the oven, accompanied by toasted slices of bread or polenta.

SWEET COURSES

Schiacciata con l'uva
GRAPE PIE

300 g risen bread dough, 150 g sugar,
1 bunch black grapes, 1 tablespoon lard,
1 tablespoon butter.
To complete the presentation: powdered sugar.

Knead the dough on a pastry board, add the lard and 2 tablespoons sugar, then let stand for an hour, covered with a cloth.

Wash the grapes well, then peel and remove pips from each individual grape; reserve some of the grapes and crush the others coarsely with a fork. Knead the dough again a little, then divide it into two halves and roll it with a rolling-pin into two thick discs. Use one to line the inside of a 20 cm pie pan greased with butter, then place the crushed grapes on the pastry. Dust with the sugar, then cover with the other pastry disc, pinching the edges together.

Lastly, decorate with the remaining whole grapes and bake in the oven at 200 °C for 30 minutes. When ready to serve, sprinkle the grape pie with powdered sugar.

Castagnaccio
CHESTNUT CAKE

300 g chestnut flour, 50 g pine nuts,
50 g raisins, 1 sprig rosemary,
1/4 glass extra-virgin olive oil, pinch of salt.

"Castagnaccio" is one of the most typical and time-honoured cakes. It is best when served warm.

Mix the chestnut flour in a bowl with a little water, whipping it to form a creamy batter without lumps. Add the oil, a pinch of salt, some pine nuts and some of the raisins, pre-soaked in warm water and squeezed out carefully. Mix thoroughly so that the nuts and raisins are evenly distributed throughout the batter, which should be very fluid.

Grease with olive oil a rectangular baking pan, large enough so that the batter will fill it to a height of about 2 cm.

Pour the batter in and sprinkle on it the remaining raisins and pine nuts; add a few rosemary needles. Bake in the oven at 200 °C for about 40 minutes.

The chestnut cake is done when the top is cracked but not burned. Serve warm cut in squares.

Buccellato
LEMON BREAD

400 g flour, 150 g sugar, 50 g butter, 10 g brewer's yeast,
2 eggs, grated rind of 1 organic lemon, 2 tablespoons of milk,
1 pinch of baking soda, 1 pinch of salt.

Sift the flour into a small heap, add the sugar, grated lemon rind, a pinch of salt and baking soda. Then add the eggs, the butter that has been softened at room temperature and cut into pieces, and the brewer's yeast dissolved in a little milk. Knead the dough with your hands until it is smooth and compact, then cover with a clean cloth and allow to stand for about two hours.

After this time, knead it again before placing in a buttered and floured 18-20 cm pie dish. Bake in the oven at 180 °C for 40 minutes.

Serve the buccellato cold, accompanied by cream or home-made jam, or by a glass of very fine Vin Santo to dip the slices in.

Pasticcini fiorentini
FLORENTINES

*150 g butter, 150 g sugar, 150 g shelled and peeled almonds,
7 tablespoons cream, 2-3 tablespoons liquid honey,
1 tablespoon butter.
Garnish: 1 bar of semi-sweet chocolate,
cherries in syrup.*

Chop half of the almonds and cut the remaining half into wafer-thin slices. Put the butter, cream, honey and sugar together in a pan, place over moderate

heat and cook for about ten minutes, stirring with a wooden spoon until the sugar begins to caramelise.

Add the almonds to the mixture and mix well. Scoop small heaps of the mixture onto a well greased oven tray, using a spoon dipped into cold water before each scoop. Take care not to place the little heaps too close to one another, as these delicate almond biscuits may run into each other and crumble. When they are arranged on the tray, flatten each one a little on top with the spoon. Bake at about 180 °C, placing the tray on the highest rack in the oven, for 15-20 minutes. Remove the tray from the oven and detach the biscuits carefully. Meanwhile cut the cherries into small pieces and dissolve the chocolate over simmering water. When the chocolate has melted, combine it with the chopped cherries. Spread a thick layer of this chocolate mixture on the lower side of the cookies, and set to dry on a rack upside down.

Cotognata
QUINCE JELLY

5 kg quinces, 1 kg Rennet apples,
oranges and lemons totalling 1 kg, 1 stick vanilla,
granulated sugar as needed, 1 glass of bourbon or brandy.

Cotognata is a kind of jelly made of quinces. Quince trees produce a highly fragrant fruit, sharp-tasting and with an elevated pectin content, making it ideal for jelly, as pectin is a natural gelatinizing substance. Wash and cut the apples and quinces into pieces, place in a pot, preferably earthenware, and cook over moderate heat. When they begin to ooze juice, add the peeled and sliced oranges and lemons. Cook over moderate heat for about 2 hours.

Then pass the fruit through a sieve, weigh the resulting pulp and add the same amount of sugar as the weight of the pulp. Return the fruit to heat, adding the vanilla and the brandy (or bourbon), and boil for 1 hour. Remove from heat and, while still hot, pour in moulds lined with greased paper. Fill each mould to the height of about 2 cm, then cover with aluminum foil. Leave the moulds in a cool place for about ten days, then the jam is ready to use.

Crogetti
CITRUS FRITTERS

(For 10/15 people) 1 kg flour, 400 g sugar, 200 g butter, 10 eggs,
zest and peel of 2 organic lemons and 2 organic oranges,
1 small glass of rum, 1 small glass of Rosolio liqueur,
2 sachets vanilla-flavoured baking powder, vanilla-flavoured
powdered sugar, 1 pinch salt.
For deep-pan frying: sunflower oil or extra-virgin olive oil.

Crogetti are the typical fritters of the Carnival period in southern Tuscany. Sift the flour into a heap on the kitchen counter, add the eggs, melted butter, sugar, a small pinch of salt, the grated lemon and orange rind (without the pith) and the liqueur. Delicately knead the pastry, and as soon as it begins to stick together, add the vanilla-flavoured baking powder. Continue to knead until a smooth paste is obtained, then roll the dough with the rolling pin into a sheet of pastry that is not too thin. Cut it into lozenges and fry in boiling oil. As soon as they turn golden brown, drain and let dry on paper towels. Serve with a dusting of powdered sugar.

Panforte
SPICE CAKE

*450 g of peeled almonds, 350 g of candied fruit,
250 g of walnut kernels, 350 g of sugar, 100 g of honey,
2-3 ground cloves, nutmeg, cinnamon, 1 tablespoon of flour,
2 tablespoons of powdered sugar, edible rice-paper.*

Dissolve the sugar and honey in a saucepan over low heat, stir carefully to prevent the syrup from sticking. When it has the right consistency, remove from the heat and add the chopped walnuts and candied fruit, toasted almonds, an abundant pinch of cinnamon and ground cloves, a sprinkling of nutmeg, and the flour. Pour the mixture on a slab of marble or a wet tray and spread out to a thickness of approximately 2 cm; mould into a rounded shape and attach strips of oven paper lined with the rice-paper around the edges. Cook in the oven at low heat for about half an hour. Remove from the oven and when cool dust with powdered sugar and nutmeg. Arrange on a serving plate, remove the paper and cut off any uneven parts of the rice-paper at the base.

Cantuccini di Prato
ALMOND BISCUITS PRATO-STYLE

300 g flour, 200 g sugar, 100 g shelled and peeled sweet almonds,
3 eggs, 1/2 organic orange, 1 tablespoon anise seed, 1/2 glass of
milk, pinch of baking soda, pinch of salt, butter to grease the oven tray.

Sift the flour into a heap on the pastry board together with the baking soda. Slowly add the sugar, pinch of salt, 1 teaspoon of grated orange peel after removing the pith, the anise seed and almonds. Break 2 eggs into these ingredients and work together carefully, adding a drop of milk if the dough is too stiff. Then shape into 3 elongated rolls about 5 cm thick; place them on the oven tray greased with butter and brush them with the beaten yolk of the remaining egg. Bake in the oven at 190 °C for 15 minutes. Remove from the oven and cut up into slanting slices, to obtain the classic wedge shape of cantuccini. Put back in the oven for another 5 minutes.

Cenci
RAG-SHAPED FRITTERS

400 g flour, 250 g sugar,
30 g anise seed, 4 eggs, 1 pinch of powdered vanilla essence,
1 pinch of ammonium carbonate, rind of 1 organic orange,
1 glass of Vin Santo, pinch of salt.
For frying: sunflower oil or lard.
Dusting: vanilla-flavoured powdered sugar
to dust over the finished cenci.

Traditionally associated with the carnival festivities, cenci can be served either hot or cold. The quantities recommended here are sufficient for about 8 people.

Wash the anise seeds and boil with the Vin Santo for one minute, then set aside to cool, covered with a clean cloth; drain, reserving the Vin Santo. Sift the flour into a heap on the pastry board, add the eggs, the reserved Vin Santo, the sugar and a pinch of salt. Work all these ingredients together, adding the flour a little at a time to form a smooth paste. Then add a pinch of ammonium carbonate and vanilla essence and grated orange peel (without the pith), and knead well. Roll out into a thin sheet of pastry with the rolling pin, dust with a little more flour, cut into lozenge shapes using a knife or pastry cutter, and deep-fry immediately in hot oil or fat. When they are golden brown, remove from the oil and drain, placing the cenci on paper towels. Lastly, sprinkle with vanilla-flavoured powdered sugar.

Pan co' santi
WALNUT AND RAISIN LOAF

(For 10 people) 2 kg flour (type 0), 1 tablespoon butter,
200 g walnut kernels, 200 g raisins, 200 g sugar,
50 g brewer's yeast, 50 g shelled and peeled hazelnuts or almonds,
15 g powdered black pepper, 10 g salt, 2 tablespoons lard,
1 tablespoon anise seed, 1 organic lemon, 1 egg, extra-virgin olive oil.

The quantities given here are for a cake large enough for about 10 people. Chop the hazelnuts, grate the lemon rind, wash the anise seed; wash the raisins and soak them in a little water. Reserve a few walnuts and chop the rest, then sauté in a pan with the lard. Allow to cool, then add the well squeezed raisins, reserving a few for later use.

Dissolve the yeast with a few drops of warm water. Sift the flour into a small heap on the pastry board, add the dissolved yeast, the sautéed walnuts and raisins, and begin to work the ingredients together, gradually adding a few drops of warm water. When the dough begins to stick together, add the sugar, salt, pepper, almonds or hazelnuts, lemon rind (without the pith) and anise seed. Continue to knead the dough thoroughly, then set aside to rise in a wicker basket covered with a clean floured cloth. Wrap the entire basket in a blanket and leave in a warm place, away from drafts, for at least 3 hours.

Then divide the dough into balls of about 500 g each, flour them, brush them with beaten egg white and let rest for a further 30 minutes.

Then place the loaves in an oven dish, decorate with a few raisins and some walnut kernels and bake in a preheated oven at 210 °C for about 35 minutes.

Switch off the oven, open the oven door and leave open for 5 minutes, to dry the loaves completely. Remove from oven. Pan co' santi is best if left to rest for at least 24 hours before eating.

Ricciarelli di Siena

ALMOND CURLS SIENA-STYLE

250 g powdered sugar,
150 g shelled and peeled
sweet almonds,
15 g shelled and peeled
bitter almonds,
1 egg,
20 confectionery wafers.

Powder the almonds with a meat hammer or a food grinder.

Add most of the powdered sugar and mix well, then whip the egg white until stiff, and delicately fold it into the almond paste, one tablespoon at a time.

When the paste becomes too stiff to be mixed with a spoon, work it with your hands on the kitchen pastry board dusted with a little powdered sugar.

Knead until the paste is smooth, then roll out with the rolling pin to a thickness of about 1-1.5 cm, and cut into discs the size of the confectionery wafers.

Place the confectionery wafers on an oven tray and then place an almond paste disc on each wafer.

Cover with a teacloth and let rest for 1 hour in a cool place.

Bake in a preheated oven at 160 °C for about 30 minutes, without letting the biscuits brown.

Remove from the oven, allow to cool and serve with a sprinkling of powdered sugar after having trimmed off any excess wafer protruding from the almond discs.

Index of recipes
in alphabetical order

Notes